DECKS

By the Editors of Sunset Books

Sunset Books
President and Publisher: Susan J. Maruyama
Director, Sales & Marketing: Richard A. Smeby
Production Director: Lory Day
Editorial Director: Bob Doyle

Sunset Publishing Corporation
Chairman: Jim Nelson
President/Chief Executive Officer: Stephen J. Seabolt
Chief Financial Officer: James E. Mitchell
Publisher: Anthony P. Glaves
Circulation Director: Robert I. Gursha
Director of Finance: Larry Diamond
Vice President, Manufacturing: Lorinda B. Reichert
Editor, Sunset Magazine: William R. Marken

Decks was produced in conjunction with
St. Remy Press
President/Chief Executive Officer: Fernand Lecoq
President/Chief Operating Officer: Pierre Léveillé
Vice President, Finance: Natalie Watanabe
Managing Editor: Carolyn Jackson
Managing Art Director: Diane Denoncourt
Production Manager: Michelle Turbide

Staff for this Book:
Senior Editor: Heather Mills
Assistant Editors: Jennifer Ormston, Rebecca Smollett
Senior Art Director: Francine Lemieux
Art Director: Michel Giguère

Special Contributors:
Eric Beaulieu, Michel Blais, Robert Chartier, François Daxhelet,
Jean-Guy Doiron, Lorraine Doré, Dominique Gagné, Christine
M. Jacobs, Jim McRae, Geneviève Monette, Mark Pechenik,
Jacques Perrault, Judy Yelon

Book Consultants:
Richard Day
Don Vandervort

Cover:
Design: Susan Bryant
Photography: Philip Harvey
Photo Styling: JoAnn Masaoka Van Atta
Deck Design: Gary Marsh, All Decked Out, Marin, CA

Third printing January 1998
Copyright © 1996
Published by Sunset Books Inc., Menlo Park,
   CA 94025
First edition. All rights reserved, including the right
   of reproduction in whole or in part in any form.

ISBN 0-376-01079-7
Library of Congress Catalog Card Number: 95-070328
Printed in the United States

Acknowledgments
Thanks to the following:
APA—The Engineered Wood Association, Tacoma, WA
Jon Arno, Troy, MI
Association of Professional Landscape Designers, Chicago, IL
Benjamin Moore & Co., Ltd., Montreal, Que.
Bio-Wash Canada, Whistler, B.C.
Building Officials and Code Administrators International,
   Country Club Hills, IL
California Redwood Association, Novato, CA
Ann Christoph, Landscape Architect, South Laguna, CA
City of Stockton Permit Center, Stockton, CA
Deckmaster Inc., Sebastopol, CA
The Flood Company, Hudson, OH
Gilbert Whitney & Johns, Whippany, NJ
Tom Gorman, University of Idaho, College of Forestry,
   Wildlife, and Range Sciences (Forest Products Department),
   Moscow, ID
Hart Tool Co., Inc., Huntington Beach, CA
Hickson Corp. (Wolmanized wood), Smyrna, GA
International Conference of Building Officials, Seattle, WA
Macon Bureau of Inspection and Fees, Macon, GA
Giles Miller-Mead, Brome, Que.
Mobil Chemical Co. (Trex Wood-Polymer Lumber),
   Winchester, VA
National Roofing Contractors Association, Rosemont, IL
Northeastern Lumber Manufacturers Association,
   Cumberland, ME
Northwestern Steel and Wire, Sterling, IL
Osmose Wood Preserving, Inc., Griffin, GA
Powder Actuated Tool Manufacturers' Institute, Inc.,
   St. Charles, MO
PPG Architectural Finishes, Pittsburgh, PA
The Private Garden, Lake Forest, IL
ProDeck, Dallas, TX
PVC Lumber Corporation, Montreal, Que.
Simpson Strong-Tie Co., Pleasanton, CA
Southern Forest Products Association (Southern Pine Council),
   Kenner, LA
UGL Zar Products, Scranton, PA
Western Red Cedar Lumber Association, Vancouver, B.C.
Western Wood Products Association, Portland, OR
Wolman Wood Care Products, Pittsburgh, PA
ZCL Composites, Inc. (E-Z Deck), Montreal, Que.

Picture Credits
p. 4 courtesy California Redwood Association
p. 5 *(upper)* courtesy California Redwood Association
p. 6 *(both)* courtesy Western Red Cedar Lumber Association
p. 7 *(both)* courtesy Hickson Corporation (Wolmanized wood)
p. 8 *(upper)* courtesy Osmose Wood Preserving, Inc.
p. 8 *(lower)* courtesy Western Red Cedar Lumber Association
p. 9 *(both)* courtesy ProDeck
p. 10 *(upper)* courtesy California Redwood Association
p. 10 *(lower)* courtesy Hickson Corporation (Wolmanized wood)
p. 11 *(both)* courtesy Hickson Corporation (Wolmanized wood)
p. 12 *(upper)* courtesy California Redwood Association
p. 12 *(lower)* courtesy Western Wood Products Association
p. 13 *(upper)* courtesy Western Red Cedar Lumber Association
p. 13 *(lower)* courtesy Mobil Chemical Company
        (Trex Wood-Polymer Lumber)
p. 14 courtesy California Redwood Association
p. 15 *(upper)* courtesy Western Red Cedar Lumber Association
p. 15 *(lower)* courtesy Hickson Corporation (Wolmanized wood)

CONTENTS

DECK POSSIBILITIES

These days, outdoor living is an important part of many people's lives. We go outdoors to shake off daily stresses, recharge our spirits, and engage in our favorite pastimes. It's our love of the outdoors that makes decks so popular—they're comfortable, attractive, and adaptable to almost any terrain.

On the following pages, you'll find photographs of a variety of decks, from modest garden floors to spectacular cantilevered platforms. Decks with interesting details—railings, stair designs, benches, planters, screens, and overheads—are also included to spark your imagination. Let the photographs be an inspiration for your own deck planning. You can combine aspects of the various designs to create the deck that's right for you, whether you plan to build it yourself or have a professional do the work.

As you flip through the pages, keep in mind that decks must be built to conform to building code requirements, which are different from one locale to another, and which change and develop over time. Some of the decks and deck details shown here may not conform to the current building codes in your area.

Built-in benches enhance the feeling of intimacy on
this freestanding deck, creating a cozy garden retreat.
Design: Bonnie Brocker-Beaudry (Milt Charno Associates)

The unusual shape of this redwood deck is emphasized by the hexagonal decking pattern. The built-in bench provides a perfect place for reading or relaxing; movable planter boxes and fanciful railing lights complete the finely crafted design.
Design: Christopher Klos, Westbrook Klos

Built over a steep slope, this multilevel western red cedar deck extends the lot's useful recreational space. The decking runs in the same direction on both levels, giving the illusion of a seamless transition, while the tempered glass railing panels provide an uninterrupted view.

An overhead can cover the entire deck or just part of it. Supported on massive poles, this structure combines a solid cover on one side and an open rafter design on the other, providing shade for the spa and bench seating.

Its solid cover and finely detailed railing give this deck the look of a porch. The decking is laid in short spokelike sections, to follow the line of the house and emphasize the curve.

An overhead need not be solid to provide shade: An open cover such as this one will diffuse the sun's bright rays. Plants in hanging baskets can be easily removed for pruning or replanting.

A common railing design, vertical balusters between horizontal rails, is made more stylish with the addition of decorative horizontal crosspieces.

The openness of these stairs—made of spaced 2x4s on open risers—raises the deck visually. The angle of the stairs up to the deck is repeated in the angled steps up to the house, tying them together.

Covered with a gazebo-style overhead, this small deck projects like a peninsula from the main deck. The use of the same railing design—vertical balusters attached to a rail at the top and a fascia at the bottom—blends the two elements together. A series of low-voltage deck lights brightens the way at night.

Built to surround a spa, this pressure-treated wood deck includes a screen for privacy and stylish benches for lounging.

This backyard retreat has many kitchen conveniences: a sink, countertops, and cupboards, as well as post-top lighting for evening enjoyment. The tiles in the built-in benches and planters match the countertops, creating a harmonious design. Design/builder: John Hemingway

Divided into different activity areas—for sunbathing or soaking—this multilevel deck increases the usable surface of a sloping lot. Railings are required for safety on the high sides, but on the low side, a wraparound step gives easy access to the yard. The white railings are an attractive color contrast to the natural-tone decking.

More commonly built above a garage, a rooftop deck makes a splendid addition to a boathouse, turning otherwise unusable space into a recreation area.

The beauty of growing things livens up this deck: Flowers in built-in planters provide splashes of color and the tree growing through the middle of the lowest level offers natural shade. The decking is cut to accommodate the tree.

A raised section bridging the pool unites the disjointed halves of this redwood deck. The combination of wide and narrow deck boards adds style; wider boards create a visual border at poolside edges. Design/builder: BFB & Associates

Beautifully landscaped, this garden floor deck exists harmoniously with its surroundings. The zigzag edge of the upper deck emphasizes the level change and creates more usable space than a straight edge would.

These narrowly spaced balusters, grouped in clusters, provide safety with style on this high-level western red cedar deck.

A deck doesn't have to be surfaced with wood boards to look good. This decking is a composite made from reclaimed plastic and waste wood, yet it harmonizes well with the style of the house and the wood railings. These boards don't require any finish for weather protection, but they can be painted or stained to match the color scheme of any home.

Hugging the hillside, this multilevel redwood deck meanders gracefully from level to level. Built-in benches provide seating along the way, and planters offer on-deck landscaping possibilities. A lath skirt hides the substructure.
Design/builder: Gary Cushenberry

This railing's tightly spaced balusters give a sense of privacy, while the clear panels at the front allow for an uninterrupted view. The gate at the top of the stairs provides extra safety.

Wide stairs lead down a slope to this multilevel deck. The change in direction of the decking on the higher octagonal deck visually emphasizes the change in height.

DECK MATERIALS

One of the most important steps you'll undertake in designing your deck will be the selection of materials. The materials you choose will affect not only the look of your deck, but also its ease of construction, strength, and durability.

Lumber is usually the most expensive component of a deck. Becoming familiar with types of wood and lumberyard terminology can not only save you money, but also help you avoid mistakes that might shorten the life of your deck. To choose the right lumber for the job, you'll need to consider factors such as grading, moisture content, and decay resistance; these are discussed beginning on page 18.

To put all the materials together, you'll need a variety of fasteners, such as nails and screws, as well as metal connectors such as joist hangers. Starting on page 22 we'll introduce you to the most common types of fasteners and connectors and help you determine which one is appropriate for each situation.

Before you finalize your list of materials, be sure to ask about any new products that may be sold at home centers or lumberyards in your area.

Shown here are a few options in decay-resistant wood used for decking. Starting from left are two grades of redwood (Clear All Heart and Construction Heart), two grades of western red cedar (Custom Clear and Custom Knotty), and radius-edge pressure-treated southern pine.

MATERIALS OVERVIEW

Most decks are built on a foundation of concrete footings and piers, which support a structure made of wood and surfaced with wood decking. This is the type of deck we will show you how to build in this book. Below, we give you a brief overview of these most basic materials, and we'll also introduce you to some alternative materials you might want to consider for both the surface and substructure of your deck.

SURFACE MATERIALS

The traditional surface for a deck is wood, a material that is affordable, versatile, relatively lightweight, and easy to work with standard tools. To prevent decay, choose either pressure-treated lumber or naturally decay-resistant wood such as cedar or redwood heartwood, as shown in the photo opposite. (This is particularly important in a very damp area or one prone to termites.) You can vary the look of your deck surface by choosing wider or narrower boards or boards with specially milled edges. For more information on choosing lumber, turn to the next page.

For a very durable, maintenance-free deck, consider nonwood boards. These are made of a variety of materials including fiberglass composites, recycled plastic, and vinyl. Some resemble wood, while others are available in solid colors. Some nonwood decking products snap into tracks with no visible fasteners.

Another option for your deck surface is to install synthetic outdoor carpeting. This material is highly durable and provides good traction, but it will require more upkeep than other surface materials. To lay outdoor carpeting, you'll need to first install a base of pressure-treated plywood.

SUBSTRUCTURE MATERIALS

Wood is the most common material for the substructure of your deck—the posts, beams, and joists. To ensure that your deck resists decay, you'll want to choose pressure-treated lumber. For a discussion of lumber species, grades, sizes and other pertinent information, turn to the next page. If you're planning a rustic-looking deck, consider using treated poles as the posts. Custom-manufactured laminated beams are also available; they come in curved and arched shapes, and some can span up to 30 feet. However, such beams are generally limited to professionally designed decks.

Decks over sand, mud, or water should be supported with pilings. These are large diameter steel or wood poles that are driven into the ground. Pilings must be designed and installed by a professional, but once they're in place, the do-it-yourselfer can usually complete the rest of the deck.

Steel posts and beams offer exceptional strength in small dimensions. Because of its high cost, structural steel is usually used only for carrying extreme loads or for crossing unusually long spans. Steel structures must be professionally engineered; installation requires welding and often the use of special lifts or even a crane.

Most decks stand on concrete footings and piers. In some cases—when a deck is perched on a steep hillside, for example—concrete columns take the place of footings, piers, and posts. Concrete columns are usually cylindrical and formed using special fiber tubes, available at masonry supply companies and home improvement centers. The columns must be reinforced with steel bars. Though working with concrete involves hard physical labor, fairly small jobs are generally manageable. As a rule, do-it-yourselfers shouldn't attempt to cast concrete columns taller than 5 feet above grade. For information on working with concrete, turn to page 48.

ASK A PRO

HOW CAN I ACHIEVE A WATERTIGHT DECK SURFACE?
Watertight decks first require a plywood base, sloped slightly to allow for drainage. To waterproof the surface, you have a number of options. One possibility is to apply a waterproof membrane such as hot-mopped asphalt (this is best done by a professional). Once the surface has been prepared, you can install one of a number of materials, including tile, concrete pavers, brick, or a layer of concrete. You might want to consider hiring a mason for this job.

Another method of waterproofing is "glassing"; this involves putting down a special fiberglass mat and then applying coats of polyester resin. Fiberglass can be installed by the do-it-yourselfer, but it can be tricky, so be sure to follow the manufacturer's directions.

Finally, a waterproof surface can be achieved by applying a bitumen or elastomeric coating. These rubberlike surfaces form both the waterproof membrane and the final walking surface.

CHOOSING LUMBER

You'll get much better service at a lumberyard if you go in knowing exactly what you're looking for. In this section we'll introduce you to the terms used to describe the characteristics of lumber. Once you've decided what type of lumber you need and are ready to place your order, you'll need to know how lumber is sold.

Decay-resistance is a major concern in choosing lumber for outdoor applications. You'll want to select wood that is naturally decay-resistant, as discussed below, or that has been pressure-treated *(page 21)*.

LUMBER CHARACTERISTICS

The use you can make of a particular piece of lumber depends on the species, the moisture content, the way the piece is cut, and any existing defects.

Softwood and hardwood: These terms don't refer to a wood's relative hardness, but rather to the kind of tree from which it comes: Softwoods come from evergreens (conifers), and hardwoods from broadleaf (deciduous) trees. Because hardwoods are generally costlier, and more difficult to work with, they're rarely used for deck construction. (Some exotic tropical hardwoods such as ipé are decay-resistant and can be used for decking—consult your local hardwood dealer.)

Species: Wood is defined by its species, or the particular tree that it comes from. Woods of different species have different characteristics, as shown in the chart below. Douglas-fir/larch, southern yellow pine, and hem/fir are good choices for the deck substructure because of their structural strength. Redwood and cedar are common choices for decking and railings, due to their decay-resistant properties, discussed below. Pressure-treated ponderosa and red pine are excellent choices for decking; pressure-treated hem/fir and southern yellow pine are less expensive options.

Sapwood, heartwood, decay resistance: Even within a species, a wood's properties will vary depending upon which part of the tree it came from. The inactive wood nearest the center of a living tree is called heartwood. Sapwood, next to the bark, contains the growth cells. Although redwood and cedar are generally considered to be naturally decay-resistant species, it is in fact only the heartwood that is decay-resistant. Sapwood of species such as southern yellow pine is used for pressure-treated wood because it is porous and absorbs the preservatives well.

Moisture content: Lumber is either air-dried or kiln-dried to a certain percentage moisture content before it is surfaced. The moisture content of lumber dramatically

MAJOR SOFTWOODS		
Species or species group	**Growing range**	**Characteristics**
Cedar, western red	Pacific Northwest from southern Alaska to northern California; Washington east to Montana	Heartwood is similar to redwood in decay-resistance, but not as resistant to termites; coarser than redwood. High resistance to warping, weathering. Strongly aromatic. Somewhat weak and brittle; moderate nail-holding ability; very easy to work.
Douglas-fir/ western larch	Western states (Rocky Mountains and Pacific Coast ranges)	Very heavy, strong, and stiff; good nail-holding ability. Somewhat difficult to work with hand tools. Resistant to decay and termites only if pressure-treated with preservatives.
Hem/fir (eastern and western hemlock; true firs)	Western hemlock and firs: Rocky Mountains and Pacific Coast ranges; eastern hemlock: northeastern U.S. and Appalachians	Firs are generally lightweight, soft to moderately soft, with average strength. Hemlocks are fairly strong and stiff; below-average nailing ability. Firs are easy to work; hemlocks are somewhat more difficult. Shrinkage can be substantial. Resistant to decay and termites only if pressure-treated with preservatives.
Pine, ponderosa	Western states	Moderately strong and stiff; high resistance to warping. Good nail-holding ability. Not as strong as southern pine, but easier to work. Resistant to decay and termites only when pressure-treated.
Pine, red	New England, New York, Pennsylvania, and lake states	Strong and stiff. Good nail-holding ability. Not quite as strong as southern pine but easier to work. Resistant to decay and termites only if pressure-treated.
Pine, southern yellow (longleaf, slash, shortleaf, loblolly)	Southeastern U.S. from Maryland to Florida; Atlantic Coast to East Texas	Very strong and stiff, hard, good nail-holding ability. Moderately easy to work. Resistant to decay and termites only if pressure-treated with preservatives.
Redwood	Northwestern California, extreme southwestern Oregon	Heartwood known for its durability and resistance to decay, termites. Moderately lightweight with limited structural strength (but strong for its weight). Good workability, but brittle; splits easily. Medium nail-holding ability.

affects the wood's ability to hold nails and other important properties. If wood is very damp, it's more likely to split, warp, or cup as it dries. Also, if it is damp when surfaced, it will tend to shrink to smaller than the expected dimensions. S-GRN designates "green" (unseasoned) lumber with a moisture content of 20% or more. S-DRY means the moisture content is 19% or less; MC-15 lumber is dried to a moisture content of 15% or less.

Pressure treatment reintroduces a great deal of moisture into the wood; some treated wood is dried again after treatment. Redwood and cedar may be available either green or kiln-dried or both, depending on the region. Since both redwood and cedar are very stable woods, even green deck boards won't warp much as they dry.

Vertical and flat grain: Depending on the cut of the millsaw, lumber will have either parallel grain lines running the length of the boards (vertical grain), a marbled appearance (flat grain), or a combination of the two. Flat-grain lumber generally has more "figure"—the wavy patterns produced by growth rings. Vertical-grain lumber is stronger and less likely than flat-grain lumber to warp or cup, but it usually costs more.

Defects: Lumber is subject to defects due to weathering and the way the piece was milled. When choosing lumber, lift each piece and sight down the face and edges for any defects. The most common defects are shown below; also look for problems such as rotting, staining, insect holes, and pitch pockets (reservoirs of resin). Keep in mind that some boards can be salvaged by cutting off the affected part.

HOW LUMBER IS SOLD

When you order lumber from a lumberyard, you'll need to specify the dimensions, whether the lumber should be rough or surfaced, and the grade. To compare the costs of different types of lumber, or of the same type from one retailer to another, you'll also need to understand the system used to price lumber.

Rough and surfaced lumber: Surfaced lumber, which is planed smooth, is the standard for most construction and a must for decking. It is available in a range of grades (page 20). Some lumberyards also carry rough lumber, but it may be available only in lower grades.

Sizing: Be aware that a typical "2x4" is not actually 2 inches by 4 inches. The nominal size of lumber is designated before the piece is dried and surfaced; the actual size is less. Rough lumber is actually closer to the nominal dimensions. For real sizes of surfaced lumber, consult the chart on the next page.

Lumber is divided into categories based on size. *Dimension lumber* is intended for structural applications and is used for both decking and the deck substructure. Sizes range from 2 to 4 inches thick and at least 2 inches wide. *Timbers* are heavy structural lumber 5 inches thick or more used for large posts or beams. Technically, *boards* are normally not more than 2 inches thick, and are 4 to 12 inches wide. They are graded for appearance only and are used for nonstructural applications, such as planters.

Wood specifically intended for decking is available, referred to as *radius-edge patio decking*. This lumber has rounded edges and is available in actual thicknesses of 1 inch or 1⁵⁄₃₂ inch. Patio decking can also be used for amenities such as benches and planters.

Lumber is normally stocked in even lengths from 6 to 16 feet, in 2-foot increments. You may want to special-order longer pieces, if, for instance, you want to avoid end joints in your decking.

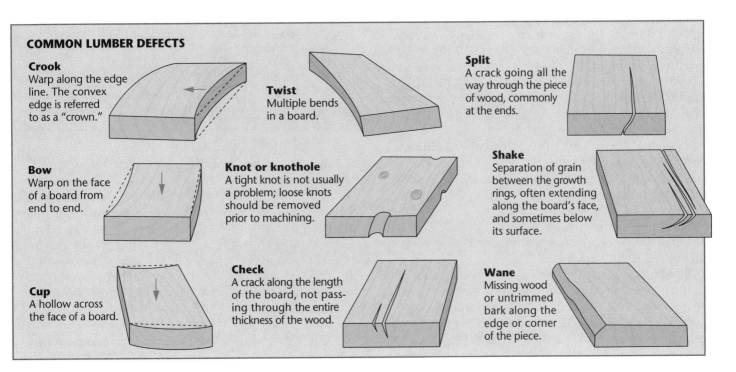

COMMON LUMBER DEFECTS

Crook
Warp along the edge line. The convex edge is referred to as a "crown."

Twist
Multiple bends in a board.

Split
A crack going all the way through the piece of wood, commonly at the ends.

Bow
Warp on the face of a board from end to end.

Knot or knothole
A tight knot is not usually a problem; loose knots should be removed prior to machining.

Shake
Separation of grain between the growth rings, often extending along the board's face, and sometimes below its surface.

Cup
A hollow across the face of a board.

Check
A crack along the length of the board, not passing through the entire thickness of the wood.

Wane
Missing wood or untrimmed bark along the edge or corner of the piece.

STANDARD DIMENSIONS OF SOFTWOODS	
Nominal size	Surfaced (actual) size
1x2	3/4"x1 1/2"
1x3	3/4"x2 1/2"
1x4	3/4"x3 1/2"
1x6	3/4"x5 1/2"
1x8	3/4"x7 1/4"
1x10	3/4"x9 1/4"
1x12	3/4"x11 1/4"
2x3	1 1/2"x2 1/2"
2x4	1 1/2"x3 1/2"
2x6	1 1/2"x5 1/2"
2x8	1 1/2"x7 1/4"
2x10	1 1/2"x9 1/4"
2x12	1 1/2"x11 1/4"
4x4	3 1/2"x3 1/2"
4x10	3 1/2"x9 1/4"
6x8	5 1/2"x7 1/4"

Architect Clear, Custom Clear, Architect Knotty, and Custom Knotty. The lower grades have more knots, but don't rule them out—you may decide you like the knotty look. Cedar grades don't indicate whether the wood is heartwood or sapwood. Cedar heartwood is a rich orange color, while the sapwood is a creamy white; if you want decay-resistant wood, pick out pieces that are all heartwood.

The top grades of redwood are the "architectural grades": Clear All Heart, Clear, B Heart, and B Grade. A more economical choice—with a rougher look—is one of the "garden grades." Of these, Construction Heart and Construction Common are suitable for decking. The lower quality garden grades—Merchantable Heart and Merchantable—are suitable for benches and planters. The grades with the word "heart" in the name are all heartwood and are therefore decay-resistant.

Radius-edge decking is graded for appearance; grading systems vary from region to region.

Grading: Lumber is sorted and graded at the mill. Generally, lumber grades depend on several factors: natural growth characteristics (such as knots), defects resulting from milling errors, and commercial drying techniques that affect each piece's strength, durability, and appearance. A stamp on the lumber identifies moisture content when the lumber was surfaced, grade, and species, as well as the producing mill and the grading agency, such as WWP for the Western Wood Products Association stamp shown at right. (Note that pressure treatment does not affect the grade.)

Dimension lumber and timbers are graded for strength. The most common grading system includes the grades Select Structural, No. 1, No. 2, and No. 3, with Select Structural being the highest grade. Often, lumberyards sell a mix of grades called "No. 2 and Better." A second grading system exists for some lumber, and includes: Construction, Standard, and Utility. A mixture of grades called "Standard and Better" is commonly available; it is less strong than No. 2 and Better. In the case of No. 2 and Better, and Standard and Better, you may be able to look through the pile to choose lumber of a slightly higher grade.

No. 2 and Better is the minimum grade required for a deck's substructure, but you may want to choose a higher grade such as Select Structural for even greater strength. For decking, either No. 2 and Better, or Standard and Better are adequate; for appearance you may want to invest in a higher grade.

"Boards" are graded for appearance. For outdoor applications, you should choose No. 2 and Better Common, or if you want to economize, No. 3 Common.

Western red cedar and redwood decking are generally graded for appearance. Each has its own grading system. The cedar grades, starting with the highest quality, are:

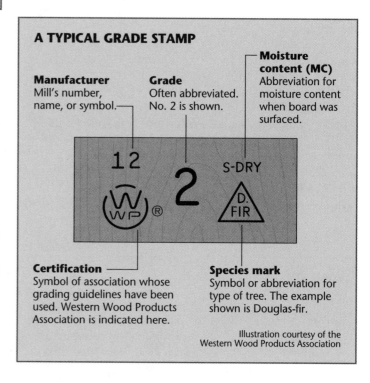

A TYPICAL GRADE STAMP

Manufacturer
Mill's number, name, or symbol.

Grade
Often abbreviated. No. 2 is shown.

Moisture content (MC)
Abbreviation for moisture content when board was surfaced.

Certification
Symbol of association whose grading guidelines have been used. Western Wood Products Association is indicated here.

Species mark
Symbol or abbreviation for type of tree. The example shown is Douglas-fir.

Illustration courtesy of the Western Wood Products Association

Pricing: The price of lumber is calculated either by the lineal foot or by the board foot. The lineal foot refers to only the length of a piece. For example, if you ask for "20 pieces of 2x4, 8 feet long" you'll be charged for 160 lineal feet of 2x4.

The board foot, on the other hand, takes all the board's dimensions into account: A piece of wood 1 inch thick by 12 inches wide by 12 inches long equals one board foot. The board foot is the most common unit for volume orders and allows you to compare pricing of different sizes of lumber. To compute board feet, use this formula: nominal thickness in inches, multiplied by nominal width in feet, multiplied by length in feet. For example, a 2x6 board 10 feet long would be computed: 2" x ¹/₂' x 10'= 10 board feet. Of course, you still need to list the exact dimensions of the lumber you need so your order can be filled correctly.

PRESSURE-TREATED LUMBER

The pressure-treating process forces chemicals into the wood to protect it against decay and termites; it is much more effective than a do-it-yourself brush-on product (although you'll still need some of this to treat sawcuts and drilled holes in the pressure-treated lumber). The preservatives most commonly used for pressure-treating are inorganic arsenicals such as chromated copper arsenate (CCA) and ammoniacal copper arsenate (ACA), also known as water-borne preservatives. Some salvaged wood, such as railway ties, has been treated with creosote, a more toxic product, and one that is hazardous to children and pets.

Pressure-treated wood is available in two exposures, depending on the amount of preservative: Ground Contact is required for lumber that will be close to the ground. For other applications, such as decking, you can choose Above Ground.

Working with pressure-treated wood has certain disadvantages. Due to the treatment process, it is quite damp and tends to warp as it dries; you may want to look for the type dried after treatment. Many people dislike the typically brown or greenish cast of pressure-treated wood, and some types are covered with staple-like treatment incisions (but most species are available without the incisions). Finally, special safety precautions are required for working with treated wood *(page 53).*

(page 53).

ASK A PRO

WHEN DO I NEED TO CHOOSE DECAY-RESISTANT WOOD?

Wood that traps water will decay in time. Any part of your deck that is in contact with concrete or within 6 inches of the ground must be made of decay-resistant wood. This can be either pressure-treated wood, or naturally decay-resistant wood such as redwood or cedar heartwood. For maximum durability, make your entire deck of decay-resistant wood. This is a particularly good idea in damp climates and in areas prone to termites.

Redwood and cedar are attractive options—they look good, are very stable, and are easier to nail than species that are commonly pressure-treated. However, both tend to be softer and weaker than woods such as hem/fir or southern pine, which are available pressure-treated. The decay-resistant cedar or redwood hardwood is also more expensive than pressure-treated wood and in many areas is hard to find in large sizes. To get the best of both worlds, most professional designers favor pressure-treated woods for a deck's substructure, but then opt for decking, benches, and railings of cedar or redwood heartwood. To reduce costs, the decking can be made of pressure-treated wood.

ESTIMATING AND ORDERING LUMBER

Estimating is simply a matter of measuring and counting the number of pieces necessary for your project. Ballpark estimates made early in the planning stage will help you compare the costs of different surface and substructure arrangements; a detailed estimate of your final plan provides a basis for ordering materials. Always order 5% to 10% more than your estimate to allow for waste.

For decking, the following formula will help you calculate how many boards of a specific width will cover the deck's width, assuming a standard ³/₁₆-inch spacing between planks:

Number of 2x4s laid flat = 3.3 x width of deck in feet

Number of 2x6s laid flat = 2.1 x width of deck in feet

Number of 2x2s or edge-laid 2x3s or 2x4s = 7.1 x width of deck in feet

In estimating, round your result to the next highest foot. For example, if you want to cover a 12-foot-wide deck with 2x4s, you'll need 3.3 x 12 = 39.6 boards—so you would order at least 40 boards.

No handy rules are available for estimating the amounts needed for a deck's substructure; you'll have to make your estimates by counting the pieces in your drawings.

Remember these basic rules that will help you cut the cost of materials:
1) Order as many of the materials as possible at a single time from a single supplier;
2) Choose your supplier on the basis of competitive bids from several retailers;
3) Order your lumber in the regularly available, standard dimensions.

Keep in mind that if all or part of your construction is being done by a contractor, he or she may arrange to purchase materials for you at a professional discount.

FASTENERS AND CONNECTORS

Good quality fasteners and connectors are key to a strong and durable deck. To attach your deck boards you can choose nails or screws, or special hidden deck clips. (For diagrams of fastener locations for decking, turn to page 68.) Although the substructure of your deck can be put together with nails, metal framing connectors make for much stronger joints.

Fasteners and connectors used outdoors are subject to moisture, and must be corrosion-resistant.

NAILS

The fastest and cheapest way to fasten wooden decking to joists or beams is by nailing. You can use common nails, but to avoid nail popping, deformed shank nails are a much better choice. These include the spiral and ring shank nails shown opposite. The one drawback to this type of nail is that they are hard to remove if bent; however, the increased holding power more than compensates for this inconvenience.

Use common nails to assemble your substructure. The slightly thinner box nails are a good choice for light work such as lattice or trim—they have less tendency to split the wood. For connections where you don't want a nail's head to show—and where strength isn't required—choose casing nails. After driving the nails nearly flush, sink the slightly rounded heads with a nailset.

Buy galvanized, aluminum, or stainless steel nails; other types will rust. Hot-dipped nails are the best quality galvanized nails; others such as electroplated nails have a thinner coating and are more likely to stain the decking. In fact, even the best hot-dipped nail will rust in time, particularly at the exposed head where the coating has been battered by your hammer. Stainless steel and aluminum nails won't rust, but they're hard to find (you'll probably have to special-order them) and cost about three times as much as galvanized nails. Aluminum nails are softer than the other types, and tend to bend or pop.

Nails are sold in boxes (1, 5, or 50 pounds) or loose in bins. The length is indicated by a "penny" designation (abbreviated as "d"). The equivalents in inches are shown below. To fasten decking, use 3¼-inch or 3½-inch nails.

HOW MANY NAILS PER POUND?			
	Common	Box	CASING
2½"	106	145	147
2¾"	96	132	-
3"	69	121	108
3¼"	64	94	-
3½"	49	71	71

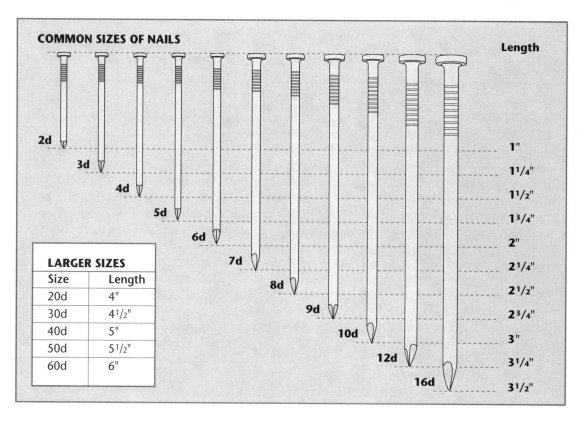

COMMON SIZES OF NAILS

LARGER SIZES	
Size	Length
20d	4"
30d	4½"
40d	5"
50d	5½"
60d	6"

Length:
2d — 1"
3d — 1¼"
4d — 1½"
5d — 1¾"
6d — 2"
7d — 2¼"
8d — 2½"
9d — 2¾"
10d — 3"
12d — 3¼"
16d — 3½"

To order nails, estimate how many you'll need from your plans and then convert to pounds, using the chart opposite. In some cases, a hardware staffperson may be able to make the estimate for you from your plans. For the nailing pattern for decking, turn to page 68.

SCREWS

Although more expensive than nails, galvanized deck screws (similar to drywall screws) provide secure, high-quality fastening for decking. Screws have several advantages over nails: They hold very securely, their galvanized coating is less likely to be damaged during installation, and they eliminate the problem of hammer dents.

Screws are sold by the pound or, at a substantial saving, by the 25-pound box. Be sure to choose galvanized screws (some even better coatings such as ceramic are also available at greater cost). The screws should be long enough to penetrate joists at least as deep as the decking is thick (for 2x4 or 2x6 decking, buy 3-inch screws).

ADHESIVES

To prevent deck boards from working loose, you can use adhesive in addition to nails or screws. However, the disadvantage of doing this is that the boards will be very difficult to remove later, for repairs.

There are some adhesives designed specifically for decking, but you can choose any construction adhesive that is appropriate for outdoor use. If you are using pressure-treated wood, make sure the adhesive is compatible with this type of wood.

HIDDEN FASTENERS

Special hidden fastening systems are available for decking. Both the deck clips and deck track shown below result in a beautiful deck with an unmarred surface. There are no nail holes or hammer dents, and no popped nails to trip on. However, both systems are more time-consuming to install than nails or screws.

The deck clips secure each board to the joist before the next one is added. With the deck track system, the track is nailed to the side of the joist near the top; the underside of each deck board is then screwed to the track.

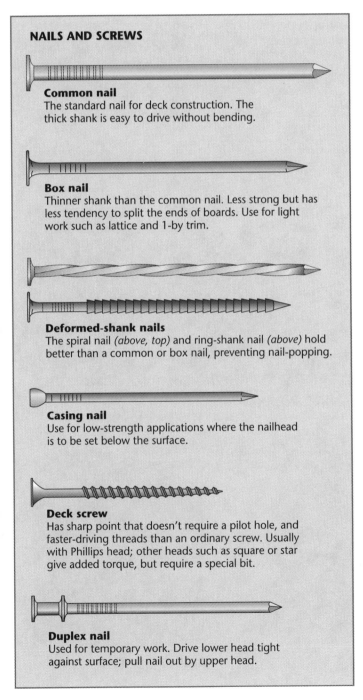

NAILS AND SCREWS

Common nail
The standard nail for deck construction. The thick shank is easy to drive without bending.

Box nail
Thinner shank than the common nail. Less strong but has less tendency to split the ends of boards. Use for light work such as lattice and 1-by trim.

Deformed-shank nails
The spiral nail (*above, top*) and ring-shank nail (*above*) hold better than a common or box nail, preventing nail-popping.

Casing nail
Use for low-strength applications where the nailhead is to be set below the surface.

Deck screw
Has sharp point that doesn't require a pilot hole, and faster-driving threads than an ordinary screw. Usually with Phillips head; other heads such as square or star give added torque, but require a special bit.

Duplex nail
Used for temporary work. Drive lower head tight against surface; pull nail out by upper head.

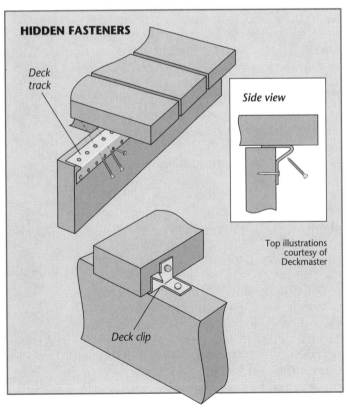

HIDDEN FASTENERS

Deck track

Side view

Deck clip

Top illustrations courtesy of Deckmaster

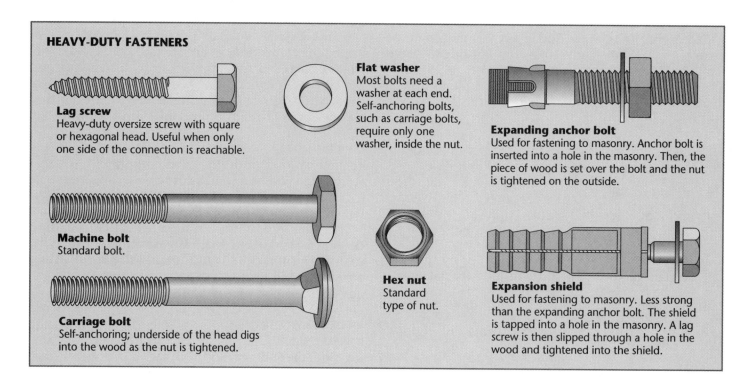

HEAVY-DUTY FASTENERS

Lag screw
Heavy-duty oversize screw with square or hexagonal head. Useful when only one side of the connection is reachable.

Machine bolt
Standard bolt.

Carriage bolt
Self-anchoring; underside of the head digs into the wood as the nut is tightened.

Flat washer
Most bolts need a washer at each end. Self-anchoring bolts, such as carriage bolts, require only one washer, inside the nut.

Hex nut
Standard type of nut.

Expanding anchor bolt
Used for fastening to masonry. Anchor bolt is inserted into a hole in the masonry. Then, the piece of wood is set over the bolt and the nut is tightened on the outside.

Expansion shield
Used for fastening to masonry. Less strong than the expanding anchor bolt. The shield is tapped into a hole in the masonry. A lag screw is then slipped through a hole in the wood and tightened into the shield.

BOLTS AND LAG SCREWS

For connections where strength is vital and where framing connectors are not used (such as ledger-to-house), the fasteners of choice are bolts or lag screws.

For decks, you'll be using 3- to 12-inch-long fasteners with diameters from $1/4$ to $3/4$ inch (diameter increases in $1/16$-inch increments). To accommodate the necessary washers and nuts, bolts should be about 1 inch longer than the combined thickness of the pieces to be bolted together. Drill holes for bolts with a bit the same diameter as the bolt. Use washers under all nuts and under the heads of machine bolts; don't use them under carriage bolt heads, since the shoulder of this type of bolt bites into the wood, keeping the bolt from turning.

Lag screws come in equivalent sizes to bolts, and are useful if only one side of the connection is accessible. Drill a pilot hole about two-thirds the length of the lag screw, using a bit $1/8$ inch smaller in diameter than the lag screw shank. Place a washer under the head of each lag screw.

The number and size of bolts or lag screws depend upon the width of the lumber; typical combinations are shown at right. Remember: It's better to form a connection with several small-diameter bolts or lag screws than with fewer fasteners of greater diameter.

For fastening wood to masonry such as when securing a ledger to a masonry wall, use expanding anchor bolts or metal shields.

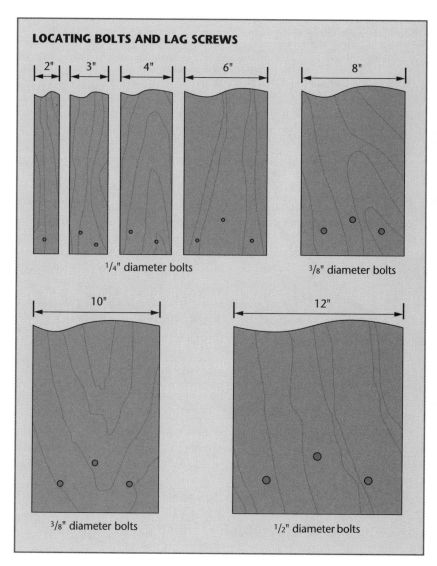

LOCATING BOLTS AND LAG SCREWS

$1/4$" diameter bolts

$3/8$" diameter bolts

$3/8$" diameter bolts

$1/2$" diameter bolts

FRAMING CONNECTORS

Although metal framing connectors add an extra cost element to your project, they will pay off in the end by making your work easier and the result stronger. They strengthen joints by allowing you to avoid the toenailing that leads to weak connections. Connectors also make it much simpler to join two pieces of wood, and they prevent splitting the ends of the lumber. Almost any home center offers most of the types of framing connectors shown below and on page 26 (and probably several others) in sizes to fit most standard dimensions of surfaced lumber. Connectors intended for outdoor use are galvanized to help prevent corrosion caused by weather.

Always use the fasteners recommended by the connector manufacturer. These are usually special short nails 1¼ or 1½ inches long to avoid complete penetration of 2-by lumber; they are thicker than ordinary nails of that length. These nails are usually available where the connectors are sold. They can be smooth-shank or ring-shank, and should be hot-dipped galvanized. In general, use all the available nail holes in the connector. Wood screws of the same diameter as the recommended nails can be used instead.

In some cases, connectors come with large holes for through bolts in addition to the small holes for nails—use one or the other as you prefer (nails are generally faster to install). With connectors that attach to only one side of the lumber, such as the stair angle shown on the next page, lag screws can be used instead of nails or bolts.

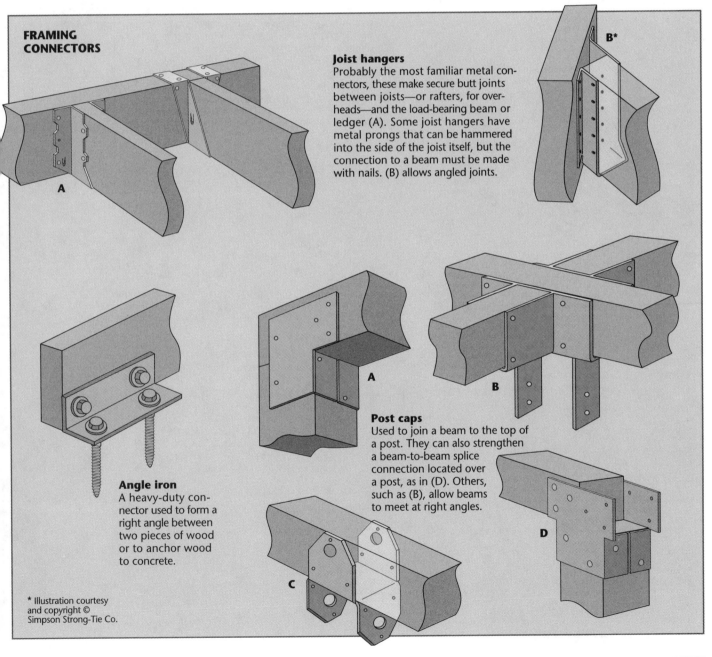

FRAMING CONNECTORS

Joist hangers
Probably the most familiar metal connectors, these make secure butt joints between joists—or rafters, for overheads—and the load-bearing beam or ledger (A). Some joist hangers have metal prongs that can be hammered into the side of the joist itself, but the connection to a beam must be made with nails. (B) allows angled joints.

Angle iron
A heavy-duty connector used to form a right angle between two pieces of wood or to anchor wood to concrete.

Post caps
Used to join a beam to the top of a post. They can also strengthen a beam-to-beam splice connection located over a post, as in (D). Others, such as (B), allow beams to meet at right angles.

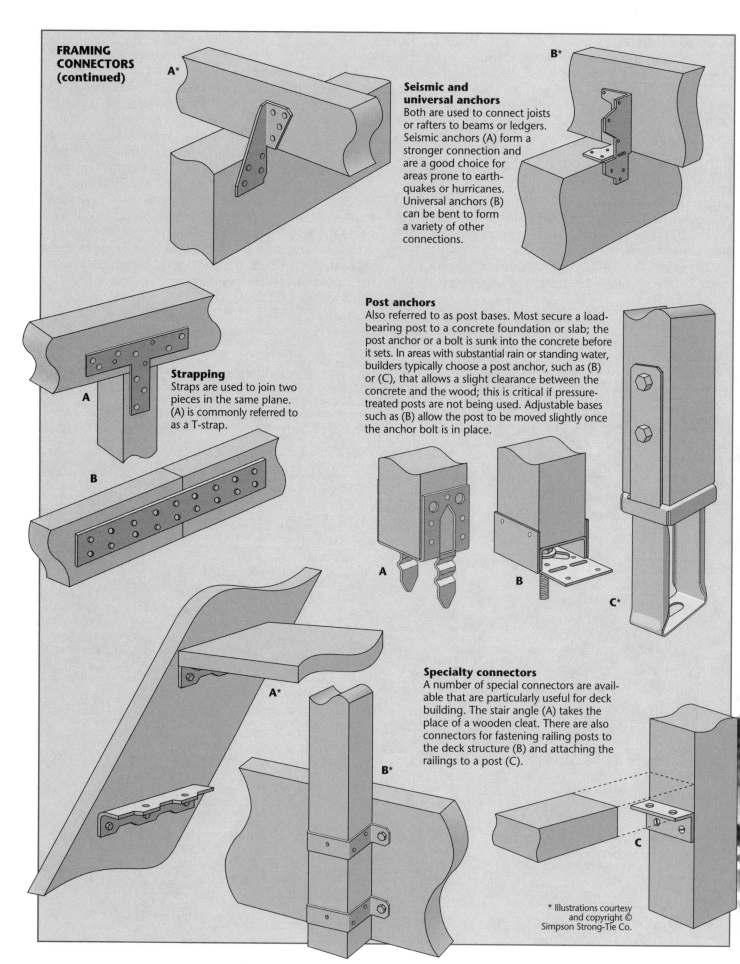

FRAMING CONNECTORS (continued)

A*

B*

Seismic and universal anchors

Both are used to connect joists or rafters to beams or ledgers. Seismic anchors (A) form a stronger connection and are a good choice for areas prone to earthquakes or hurricanes. Universal anchors (B) can be bent to form a variety of other connections.

Strapping

Straps are used to join two pieces in the same plane. (A) is commonly referred to as a T-strap.

A

B

Post anchors

Also referred to as post bases. Most secure a load-bearing post to a concrete foundation or slab; the post anchor or a bolt is sunk into the concrete before it sets. In areas with substantial rain or standing water, builders typically choose a post anchor, such as (B) or (C), that allows a slight clearance between the concrete and the wood; this is critical if pressure-treated posts are not being used. Adjustable bases such as (B) allow the post to be moved slightly once the anchor bolt is in place.

A

B

C*

Specialty connectors

A number of special connectors are available that are particularly useful for deck building. The stair angle (A) takes the place of a wooden cleat. There are also connectors for fastening railing posts to the deck structure (B) and attaching the railings to a post (C).

A*

B*

C

PLANNING YOUR DECK

Like any do-it-yourself project, building a deck requires careful thought and planning to make sure the structure you create meets the needs of your family. You'll want to consider how your family will use the deck—for entertaining, dining, or sunning, for instance. This information will help you decide on the size, shape, and location of the deck. Before you determine its exact location, you'll have to consider the microclimate of your property, as discussed on the next page, as well as any legal restrictions that may apply to your lot.

The next step is to develop working plans. We'll take you through the process, starting on page 31. To decide on a final design, you'll need to consult the chapter beginning on page 36 to learn about the components of a deck and how they are put together.

You may want to enlist the help of a professional for some part of the design or construction of your deck; turn to page 34 for tips on hiring and working with professionals.

To make your deck more comfortable and convenient to use, you may want to add amenities such as benches, storage areas, screens, or overheads; for information on these structures, turn to the chapter starting on page 79.

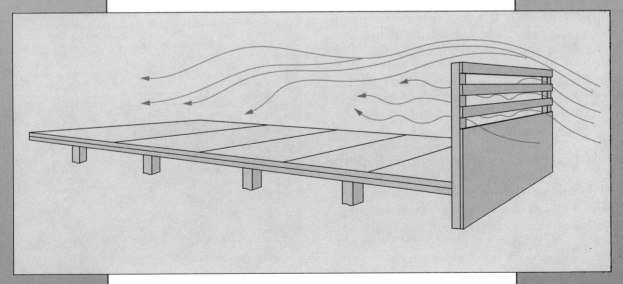

In a windy area, you can protect your deck with screens. A screen of spaced wood slats as shown here will effectively diffuse wind.

CHOOSING A SITE

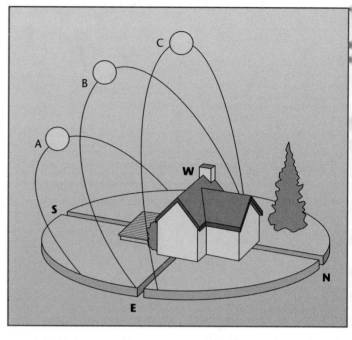

Locating your deck may seem like a straightforward decision—you might simply want it off the back door of your house—but there are many factors to consider. A deck should be conveniently accessible from both the house and the yard; consider how the proposed location and shape will affect traffic patterns. You'll also want to consider what you can see from the proposed site, as well as who can see you. Using a ladder, if necessary, check the views from various points in the yard. Keep in mind that a high-level deck can block views from the house as well as shading the area it overhangs.

Before deciding on a final location, consider the microclimate of your lot—the exposure of your deck to sun, wind, and precipitation will be affected by its proximity to buildings and trees. Microclimates will also play a role in the actual design of the deck; you may want to add an overhead for shade or screens to moderate winds.

SUN AND SHADE

In general, a deck that faces north is cool because the sun rarely shines on it, while a south-facing deck is usually warm because the sun never leaves it, from sunrise to sunset. Yards with an eastern exposure stay cool, receiving only morning sunlight; west-facing areas can be uncomfortably hot, since they absorb the full force of the sun's mid-afternoon rays.

These general rules aren't without exceptions, though. For example, in hot regions of the country, there may be north-facing decks that could hardly be considered cool in summer.

The sun crosses the sky in an arc that changes slightly every day, becoming lower in winter and higher in summer *(right, above)*. In the dead of winter, it briefly tracks across the sky at a low angle, throwing long shadows; on long summer days, it moves overhead at a very high angle. As you move farther north from the equator, the difference becomes more dramatic. To determine where the sun will fall on potential deck locations at various times of year, first find your location on the map at right, then refer to the chart for sun angles.

If you live in an area with hot summers and cold winters, shade may be welcome in summer, but not in winter. A deciduous tree will provide shade for a deck when the sun is high in the summer sky, but allow sunlight through in winter when the sun is lower and the leaves have fallen. An overhead, particularly one covered with vines, will function the same way.

SEASONAL SUN ANGLES (see illustration above)	SUN'S POSITION/ HOURS OF DAYLIGHT (see map below)		
Season	Area 1	Area 2	Area 3
A) Noon, 12/21	21°/8 hrs.	29°/9 hrs.	37°/10 hrs.
B) Noon, 3/21 and 9/21	45°/12 hrs.	53°/12 hrs.	60°/12 hrs.
C) Noon, 6/21	69°/16 hrs.	76°/15 hrs.	83°/14 hrs.

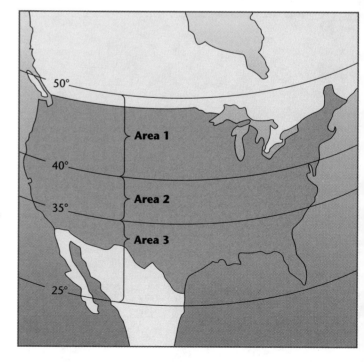

WIND PATTERNS

Too much wind can create enough chill on cool days to make a deck unusable. Likewise, if there's no breeze at all, decks in sunny locations can be very uncomfortable in summer weather.

Three different kinds of winds may affect your decision regarding your deck's placement or design: annual prevailing winds, very localized seasonal breezes, and occasional high-velocity winds generated by stormy weather. Even if your proposed deck will face strong winds only occasionally, you may have to strengthen its foundations and substructure. If it will receive mild prevailing breezes, you may wish to modify their effects with vertical screens, as illustrated in the drawings below. Note that a solid vertical barrier may not be the best choice; angled baffles, lattice-type screens, or deciduous plantings will disperse wind better. To determine which areas need to be sheltered from the wind, post small flags or ribbons at various places on your proposed site, and take note of their movements during windy periods.

Your house itself can serve as a formidable windbreak. Where regular breezes are a problem, you can shelter your deck by locating it on the side of the house opposite the direction of prevailing winds.

RAIN AND SNOW

Though you're unlikely to use your deck during poor weather, it will take a beating—and age more rapidly—if it's pounded by frequent rains. You may want to locate your deck where the house will shelter it from the weather.

As you evaluate different locations for your deck, note which way your house's roof is pitched; that's where runoff might occur. If necessary, runoff can be redirected with gutters. For information on weatherproof finishes to protect your deck from the elements, turn to page 87.

In areas that experience heavy snowfall, even if only sporadically, any deck must be capable of handling the snow's added weight. Snow is surprisingly heavy; piled 5 to 6 feet deep, it can weigh as much as 80 to 100 pounds per square foot. This standing weight alone can be enough to collapse an improperly designed structure. Make sure you follow all code requirements for your region when planning and constructing your deck. Though code requirements may not cover the strength of the deck's railings, the railings must be made sturdy enough to support the snow load.

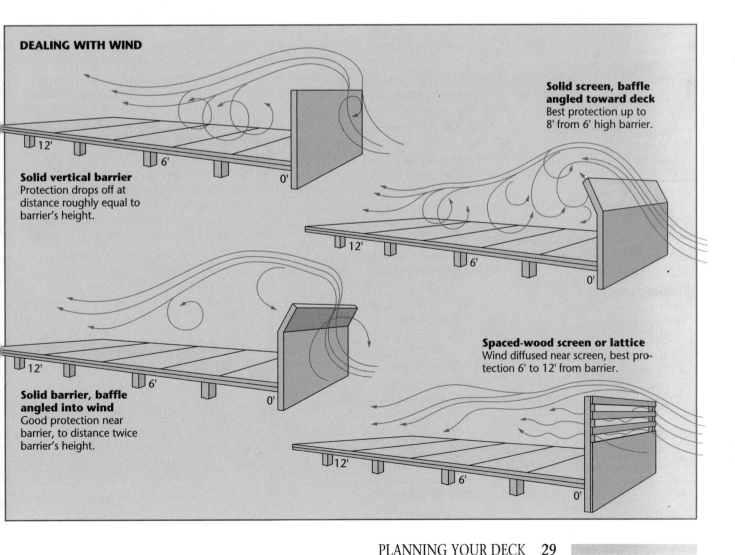

DEALING WITH WIND

Solid vertical barrier
Protection drops off at distance roughly equal to barrier's height.

Solid screen, baffle angled toward deck
Best protection up to 8' from 6' high barrier.

Solid barrier, baffle angled into wind
Good protection near barrier, to distance twice barrier's height.

Spaced-wood screen or lattice
Wind diffused near screen, best protection 6' to 12' from barrier.

Before you've gone too far in planning your deck, consult your local building department for any legal restrictions. In most areas, you'll need to file for a building permit and comply with building code requirements. Also be aware of local zoning ordinances, which normally govern whether or not a deck can be built on your land and where it can be located.

Building permits: Before you pound a single nail, get the needed permits. It's important that the building department check plans before construction begins, to ensure that you don't get off to a substandard start. Negligence may come back to haunt you: Officials can fine you and require you to bring an illegally built structure up to standard or even to dismantle it entirely.

The need for a permit generally hinges on a deck's size and intended use, and on whether or not it's attached to the house. In most areas, any deck more than 30 inches off the ground requires a permit and must be built according to building codes. If the project includes any electrical wiring or plumbing, you may need a separate permit for each of these.

Fees are usually charged for permits. These fees are generally determined by the projected value of the improvement—so when you apply for a permit, be as accurate as possible about the estimated cost. If you overestimate, you might push the fee higher. Many building offices figure a project's value based on standardized construction costs per square foot.

Building codes: Code requirements vary from region to region. They set minimum safety standards for materials and construction techniques: depth of footings, size of beams, and proper fastening methods, for example. Code requirements help ensure that any structures you build will be well made and safe for your family and any future owners of your property.

Zoning ordinances: These municipal regulations restrict the height of residential buildings, limit lot coverage (the proportion of the lot a building and other structures may cover), specify setbacks (how close to the property lines you can build), and—in some areas—stipulate architectural design standards.

Decks rarely exceed height limitations, but they're often affected by setback requirements. They also increase your overall lot coverage—an important consideration, since a new deck might limit future additions to your home.

Variances: If the zoning department rejects your plans, you can apply for a variance at your city or county planning department. It's your task to prove to a hearing officer or zoning board of appeal that following the zoning requirements precisely would create "undue hardship," and that the structure you want to build will not negatively affect your neighbors or the community. If you plead your case convincingly, you may be allowed to build.

Architectural review boards: Neighborhoods with tight controls may require that your improvement meet certain architectural standards—and that means submitting your plans to an architectural review board. Going through this process can dramatically increase the time required to get your project moving.

Deeds: Your property deed can also restrict your project's design, construction, or location. Review the deed carefully, checking for easements, architectural-standard restrictions, and other limitations.

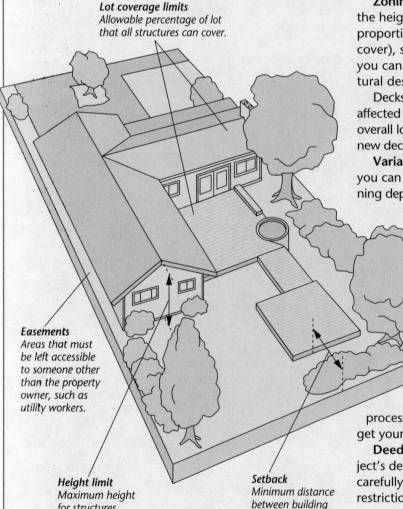

Lot coverage limits
Allowable percentage of lot that all structures can cover.

Easements
Areas that must be left accessible to someone other than the property owner, such as utility workers.

Height limit
Maximum height for structures.

Setback
Minimum distance between building or other structure and property lines.

DRAWING AND READING PLANS

If you're planning to construct your deck yourself, you'll need to develop detailed working plans. This involves a couple of preliminary steps: First, you'll have to make a general map of your house and lot, referred to as a site plan. Then you can start sketching in the overall shape of the deck. Finally, you'll be ready to draw the actual working plans showing details of the deck construction from several angles. You may decide to hire a professional for this final step. However, you'll save money and get better results if you have a site plan and sketch in hand before meeting with a designer.

DEVELOPING A SITE PLAN

Mapping your lot can be a way to make some interesting discoveries about what you thought was familiar territory. However, if you can locate the architect's drawings or deed maps that show the actual dimensions and orientation of your property, you'll save yourself considerable work. These may be available at your city hall, county office, title company, bank, mortgage company, or through the former owner. A site plan should include the following features:

Boundary lines and dimensions: Outline your property accurately and to scale, and mark its dimensions on the site plan. Indicate any required setbacks *(page 30)*. Also note the relation of the street to your house.

The house: Show your house to scale within the property. Note all exterior doors (and the direction each one opens), and all overhangs. You may also want to note the height of lower-story windows.

Exposure: Use a compass to determine North, and mark it on your plan; then note on your site plan the shaded and sunlit areas of your landscape. Indicate the direction of the prevailing winds and mark any spots that are windy enough to require shielding.

Utilities and easements: Indicate outdoor faucets and all underground lines, including the sewage line or septic tank. If you're contemplating a tall overhead or elevated deck, identify overhead lines. If your deed map shows any easements, note them and check legal restrictions limiting development of those areas.

Downspouts and drainage: Mark the locations of all downspouts and any drainage tiles, drainpipes, or catch basins. Note the direction of drainage, any point where drainage is impeded (leaving soil soggy), and any place where runoff from a steep hillside could cause erosion.

Existing plantings: If you're remodeling an old landscape, note any plantings that you want to retain or that would require a major effort or expense to remove.

Views: Note all views, attractive or unattractive, from every side of your property. Also take into account views into your yard from neighboring houses or streets.

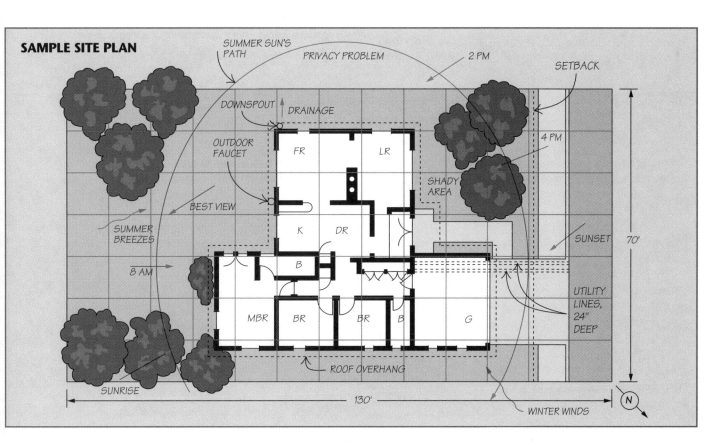

SAMPLE SITE PLAN

SUMMER SUN'S PATH · PRIVACY PROBLEM · 2 PM · SETBACK · DOWNSPOUT · DRAINAGE · 4 PM · OUTDOOR FAUCET · FR · LR · SHADY AREA · BEST VIEW · K · DR · SUMMER BREEZES · B · SUNSET · 70' · 8 AM · MBR · BR · BR · B · G · UTILITY LINES, 24" DEEP · ROOF OVERHANG · SUNRISE · 130' · WINTER WINDS · N

SKETCHING DECK CONFIGURATIONS

When you're ready to plan the shape of the deck itself, arm yourself with a good supply of tracing paper and a sharp pencil. Place a sheet of tracing paper over your site plan—you may want to enlarge the plan to make your work easier. Start by sketching some circles to indicate the basic use areas. As you work, consider such issues such as whether a children's play area is in full view of your living area, or whether the private sunning spot you envision is accessible from the master bedroom. Once you've established how you'd like to use the space, start testing possible deck configurations. Try placing scale cutouts of outdoor furniture on your sketch. If you're not pleased, just start over again with a fresh piece of paper—making changes costs nothing at this point.

When you've created a shape that seems to work, figure the deck's actual size and confirm its shape and placement at the site. Then refine your scale drawing. Finally, using a dark, felt-tip pen, draw in the permanent background—house and landscaping—on the tracing paper. Don't worry about capturing every detail—suggesting features with just a few lines should be adequate.

DEVELOPING WORKING PLANS

Once you've sketched in the overall shape of the deck, you're ready to create the working plans. To do this, you'll also have to take into account the information given in the next chapter on how a deck is put together, and you'll need to make sure the construction methods conform to any local code (page 30).

Working plans must be drawn to scale, as described below, and they should include the types of views shown opposite: plan, elevation, and details. A deck's basic surface pattern and substructure should both be drawn in plan view. The arrangement of the substructure should also be drawn in an elevation view. To simplify confusing portions of the deck, you may need to draw them in a section view as well. Railings and other vertical members are best drawn in elevation view. Attachments and other details should be drawn from the view that most clearly shows their construction; three-dimensional detail drawings sometimes work best.

Even if you don't draw up your own plans, you'll need to know how to read existing plans, such as those provided by a designer. Two simple deck plans are included in this book, starting on page 74. Remember that if you're using plans not specifically designed for your lot, you'll probably need to adjust them to suit your situation.

ASK A PRO

IS THERE SOFTWARE AVAILABLE TO HELP ME DESIGN MY DECK?

A computer drawing program is easier and more accurate than drawing by hand, and allows you to make changes easily. Software is available specifically intended for deck design. Starting from a basic deck design, the software will allow you to adapt the shape of the deck and to add features such as railings and steps. The program then allows you to view the deck from various angles. Such programs usually generate a materials list based on your design, and provide some how-to information.

DRAWING TO SCALE

To reduce the actual dimensions of your future deck to paper size accurately, you must draw it to scale. Some basic drawing tools such as a T-square, compass, protractor, and triangles will be helpful. To draw your site plan, you'll first have to measure the existing landscape. For a large lot, you may want to choose a tape measure as long as 50 to 100 feet. A long tape will reduce inaccuracies and exasperation.

For your site plan, reduce each foot of your lot to $1/4$ inch, or $1/8$ inch for a large lot. A typical scale for plan and elevation views of the deck itself is $1/4$ inch or $1/2$ inch to the foot, depending upon the deck's size. Use $1/2$ inch to the foot for details. To make the drawing job easier, you can use an architectural scale ruler. A triangular ruler such as the one shown has markings for a variety of scales.

Another way to draw to scale is to use graph paper. The most common size has $1/4$-inch squares. For a site plan, one square would be 1 or 2 feet. For plan and elevation views, one square would equal 1 foot. And for details, one square would equal 6 inches. If you need a larger drawing area than one sheet provides, tape several pieces of graph paper together.

Lower numbers are $1/4$" scale from right to left.

Upper numbers are $1/8$" scale from left to right.

DIFFERENT POINTS OF VIEW

Elevation

An elevation is a side view of the deck, revealing vertical dimensions and relationships. In the elevation shown, part of the railing has been removed to show the steps. An elevation section is a side view of a slice somewhere in the middle of the deck, often located by letters on the plan views. Elevations and elevation sections reveal vertical dimensions and relationships.

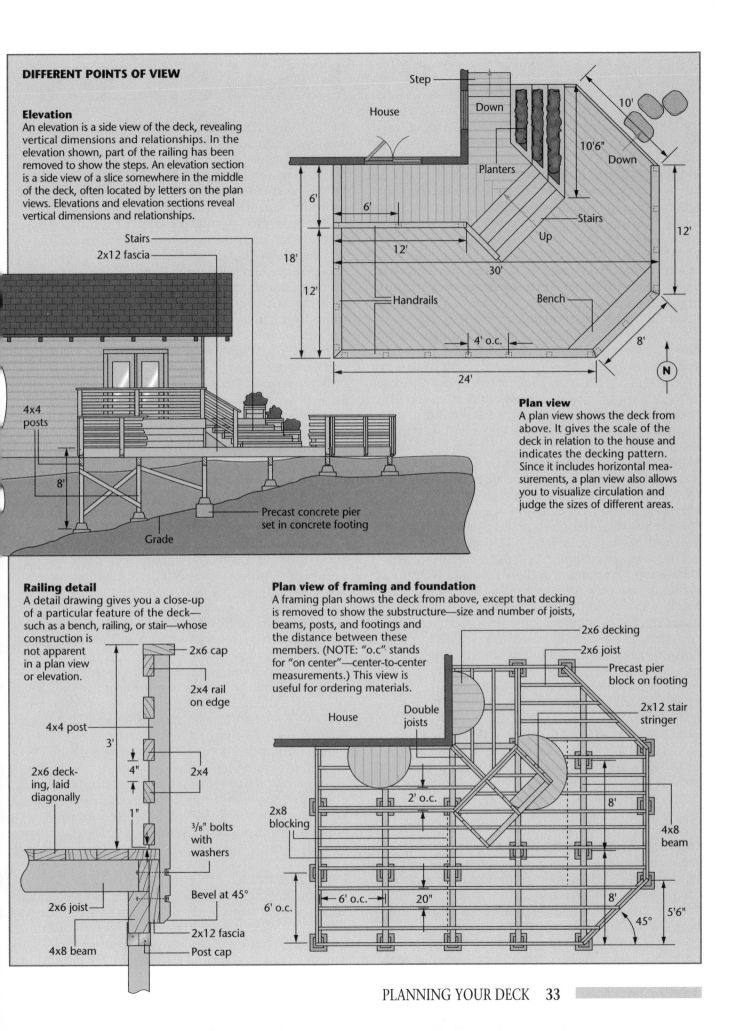

Stairs
2x12 fascia

4x4 posts

8'

Precast concrete pier set in concrete footing

Grade

Step
Down
House
Planters
Down
10'
10'6"
Stairs
12'
Up
6'
6'
12'
18'
12'
30'
Handrails
Bench
4' o.c.
8'
24'
N

Plan view

A plan view shows the deck from above. It gives the scale of the deck in relation to the house and indicates the decking pattern. Since it includes horizontal measurements, a plan view also allows you to visualize circulation and judge the sizes of different areas.

Railing detail

A detail drawing gives you a close-up of a particular feature of the deck—such as a bench, railing, or stair—whose construction is not apparent in a plan view or elevation.

2x6 cap

2x4 rail on edge

4x4 post

3'

4"

2x4

2x6 decking, laid diagonally

1"

3/8" bolts with washers

2x6 joist

Bevel at 45°

4x8 beam

2x12 fascia

Post cap

Plan view of framing and foundation

A framing plan shows the deck from above, except that decking is removed to show the substructure—size and number of joists, beams, posts, and footings and the distance between these members. (NOTE: "o.c" stands for "on center"—center-to-center measurements.) This view is useful for ordering materials.

2x6 decking

2x6 joist

Precast pier block on footing

2x12 stair stringer

House

Double joists

2' o.c.

8'

2x8 blocking

4x8 beam

6' o.c.

6' o.c.

20"

8'

45°

5'6"

WORKING WITH PROFESSIONALS

Before you launch into a deck-building project, carefully consider what part of the work you want to do yourself. Depending on your skills, you may want to hire a professional to develop plans you can work from, hire a contractor to build from plans you develop yourself, or hire professionals for both the design and construction. You can save significantly by doing your own work, but don't forget to factor in the cost of any tools you'll have to buy or rent, and expect to absorb the cost of any errors. If you do decide to hire a professional it pays to know as much as possible about deck construction so you can participate in decisions on how your deck will be designed and built.

Certain projects should be avoided. Strongly consider hiring a professional designer and/or builder if the deck you want involves any of these conditions:

• **High levels:** With decks higher than about 6 feet, it's difficult to position posts, beams, and other framing. Such decks may also require structural reinforcement to protect them from lateral loads caused by wind or earthquakes.

• **Sites over sand, mud, or water:** Decks perched above water or marshy ground, at lakeside or beach locations require special pilings for support.

• **Steep or unstable sites:** A steep site, particularly where slides may occur, must be checked by a soils engineer. A deck over such a site generally requires structural engineering and special building department approval.

• **Waterproof decking:** A deck that must be waterproof —that is, one on a roof, or one that must keep an area below it dry—requires a leak-proof barrier that's normally applied by a roofing contractor. Concrete, tile, or slate surfaces are tricky to install and best left to a masonry contractor. The added weight of such materials may require a stronger-than-normal deck structure; on a roof it may call for strengthening the roof structure.

• **Cantilevered construction:** A cantilevered deck is supported by joists or beams that extend into and are anchored by the house structure. Calculating loads for such a deck should be done by a professional.

• **Special amenities:** If your deck-building project will include electrical wiring or plumbing, or require home remodeling skills—to open up a wall, for example—you may need licensed professionals.

CHOOSING THE RIGHT PROFESSIONAL

You can choose from a variety of professionals for advice or help. Here is a brief look at some of the people who can help you and what they do.

Landscape and building architects: These state-licensed professionals can work with you to help set objectives, analyze the site, and produce detailed working plans; they can also select and estimate materials.

In addition to providing design services, some architects will negotiate bids from contractors and supervise the actual work.

Landscape architects are specialized in outdoor structures; however, if your deck poses particular engineering problems, you may want to consult a building architect. Building architects, often referred to simply as architects, design houses and have more engineering expertise than most landscape architects.

Landscape and building designers: Landscape designers often have a landscape architect's education and training, but not a state license. They can generally offer the same services as a landscape architect, and they are often more experienced with residential projects than many architects. Designers may be certified by their professional association.

Draftspersons: Drafters may be members of a skilled trade or unlicensed architects' apprentices. They can make the working plans (from which you or your contractor can work) needed for building permits.

Structural and soils engineers: Before approving your plans, your building department may require that you (or your designer) consult a structural or soils engineer. An engineer's stamp may be required if the structure will be on an unstable or steep lot, or if strong winds or heavy loads might come into play.

General and landscape contractors: Licensed general and landscape contractors specialize in construction (landscape contractors specialize in garden construction), although some have design skills and experience as well. They usually charge less for design work than landscape architects do, but some contractors may make design decisions based on ease of construction rather than aesthetics.

Contractors hired to build a small project may do all the work themselves; on a large project, they assume the responsibility for hiring qualified subcontractors, ordering construction materials, and seeing that the job is completed according to contract.

Subcontractors: If you act as your own general contractor, it's up to you to hire, coordinate, and supervise any subcontractors—specialists in grading, carpentry, plumbing, etc. Aside from following the working plans you provide, subcontractors can often supply you with current product information and sell hardware and supplies.

HIRING A DESIGNER

If you're looking for a designer, friends and neighbors are usually the best sources of information. Also contact offices of the American Institute of Architects (AIA), American Institute of Building Designers (AIBD), the American Society of Landscape Architects (ASLA), or the Association of Professional Landscape Designers (APLD), for referrals to a professional in your area. Make sure the professional has experience with small-scale residential projects. For a small project, you may also be able to entice an apprentice or draftsperson working in an architect or designer's office to draw plans for you; expect to pay by the hour.

If you include an architect or designer in your project, there are at least three working arrangements:

Retained on a consultation basis, an architect or designer will review your plans, suggest ideas for a more effective design, and perhaps provide a couple of rough conceptual sketches. After that, it will be up to you to prepare the working plans for the building department.

A second possibility is to hire a professional to design or modify your project and provide working plans for you to build from. You may be charged either a flat fee or an hourly rate.

Finally, you can retain an architect or designer on a planning-through-construction basis. Besides designing your project and providing working plans and specifications, the professional will supervise the construction process. It will cost you more to have your project designed and built this way, but you'll also be free from the plethora of details you'd have to handle otherwise.

HIRING A CONTRACTOR

In looking for a contractor, start by asking for referrals from people you know who have had similar work done. You can also ask architects and designers, local real estate brokers and lenders or even your building inspector for names of qualified builders. Experienced lumber dealers are another good source of names.

Call several contractors: First find out whether each handles your type of job and can work within the constraints of your schedule. Arrange meetings with about three of them; ask them to be prepared with photos of their work and references. Discuss your ideas or plans and ask for a rough estimate; if you have complete plans and specifications, you should be able to get firm bids. The contractor with the lowest bid will not necessarily be your best bet; look for a reasonable bid and the best credentials, references, and terms. Make sure the contractor has experience specifically with deck-building. Don't hesitate to probe for advice or suggestions that might make building your deck less expensive.

Narrow down the field to one or two contractors. Call their former clients and ask questions about quality of workmanship, communication, promptness, and follow-up. If possible, visit former clients to check the contractors' work firsthand. You can also contact the Better Business Bureau to find out whether there are existing complaints about the contractors you're considering.

Be sure your final candidate is licensed, bonded, and insured for worker's compensation, public liability, and property damage. Also try to determine how financially solvent the contractor is (you can call his or her bank and credit references for information).

HIRING WORKERS

Even if you do the work on your own, you may want to hire workers on an hourly basis. As an employer, you're expected to withhold state and federal income taxes; to withhold, remit, and contribute to Social Security; and to pay state unemployment insurance. For more information about your responsibilities as an employer, talk to a building department official, or call your state's tax department.

THE BUILDING CONTRACT

A building contract binds and protects both you and your contractor. You can minimize the possibility of misunderstandings later by writing down every possible detail. (If you're acting as your own contractor, agreements with subcontractors should be put in writing.) The contract should include all of the following:

• **The project and participants:** Include a general description of the project, its address, and the names and addresses of both you and the builder.

• **Construction materials:** Identify grade and species of lumber and quality of fasteners. Indicate brand and model number of any accessories, such as lighting systems. Avoid the clause "or equal" that will allow the builder to substitute materials for your choices.

• **Work to be performed:** Specify all major jobs from grading to finishing.

• **Time schedule:** Though a contractor cannot be responsible for construction delays caused by strikes and material shortages, he or she should assume responsibility for completing the project within a reasonable period of time. The contract should include both start and completion dates.

• **Method of payment:** Though some contractors may want a fee based on a percentage of the cost of materials and labor, it's usually wiser to insist on a fixed-price bid. Specify how payments are to be made. This is usually done in installments as phases of the work are completed. Many states limit the amount of money that contractors can request before work begins. The final payment is withheld until the job receives its final inspection and is cleared of all liens.

• **Waiver of liens:** If subcontractors are not paid for materials or services delivered to your home, in some states they can place a "mechanic's lien" on your property, tying up the title. This may happen even if the contractor is negligent. Protect yourself with a waiver of liens. Have the general contractor, subcontractors, and major materials suppliers sign it.

BUILDING YOUR DECK

In this chapter we'll show you how to build a basic deck with railings and stairs. We'll introduce you to the elements of a deck one by one, in the order you would install them. For each element, we'll present a variety of design options and then give you building instructions for the simplest, most common design. Read through this chapter carefully to see how the components of a deck all fit together.

Allow plenty of time for your project—you'll have to prepare the site; lay out the foundation; install posts, beams, and joists; and put down the decking. For information on adding amenities such as benches, screens, and overheads, as well as applying a finish, turn to the chapter starting on page 79.

Before you start to build, make sure you have all the necessary tools on hand; this chapter begins with information on the tools you're likely to need.

A deck's surface is the most visible part of a deck, and is often the easiest to install. Once the substructure is in place and you start laying the deck boards, your deck will literally take shape beneath your feet. The final touch is trimming the ends of the boards, as shown here.

TOOLS

A project as big as a deck warrants some additions to your toolkit. The tools you're likely to need are illustrated below and on the next page. In addition to those shown, you'll need some basic carpentry tools: a claw hammer; a handsaw; a caulking gun for applying both caulk and, if you're using it, adhesive. In general, buy the best-quality tools you can afford. They will make your work easier and will last longer than inexpensive equivalents.

When using a new power tool, read the owner's manual carefully and be sure to follow all safety directions. To guard against shock, power tools must be double-insulated or grounded. When using power tools outdoors, always plug them into a ground fault circuit interrupter outlet.

Before you reach for your tools, make sure you have all the necessary safety gear on hand. You'll need eye protection (goggles, safety glasses, or a face shield) when you're operating power tools. A dust mask is also essential when cutting pressure-treated wood. When applying finishes and preservatives, you'll want a respirator to protect you from the fumes; you should also wear rubber gloves when applying wood preservatives because they are harmful to the skin. Ear protection (earplugs or earmuffs) is recommended when you're using power tools for an extended period of time. Sturdy boots, preferably steel-toed, will protect your feet from dropped lumber and tools. Finally, a hard hat is a good idea when working under the deck or if you'll be working in close quarters with others.

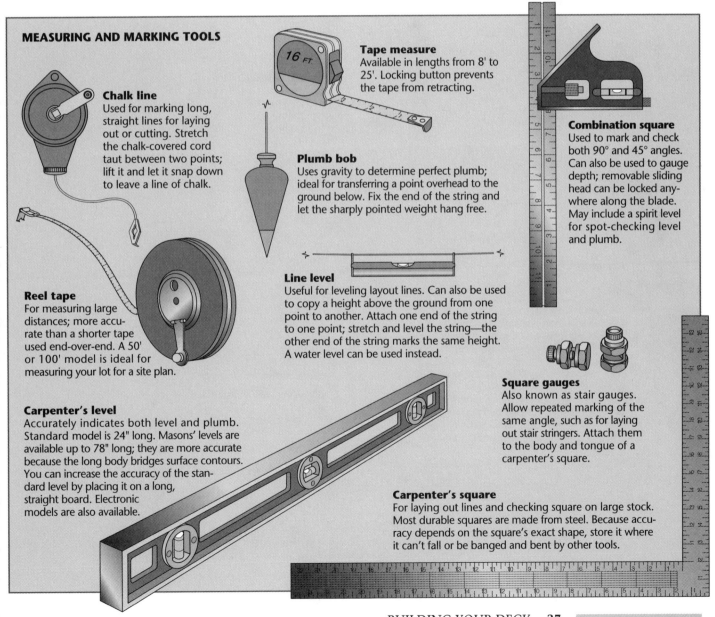

MEASURING AND MARKING TOOLS

Chalk line
Used for marking long, straight lines for laying out or cutting. Stretch the chalk-covered cord taut between two points; lift it and let it snap down to leave a line of chalk.

Tape measure
Available in lengths from 8' to 25'. Locking button prevents the tape from retracting.

Plumb bob
Uses gravity to determine perfect plumb; ideal for transferring a point overhead to the ground below. Fix the end of the string and let the sharply pointed weight hang free.

Combination square
Used to mark and check both 90° and 45° angles. Can also be used to gauge depth; removable sliding head can be locked anywhere along the blade. May include a spirit level for spot-checking level and plumb.

Reel tape
For measuring large distances; more accurate than a shorter tape used end-over-end. A 50' or 100' model is ideal for measuring your lot for a site plan.

Line level
Useful for leveling layout lines. Can also be used to copy a height above the ground from one point to another. Attach one end of the string to one point; stretch and level the string—the other end of the string marks the same height. A water level can be used instead.

Square gauges
Also known as stair gauges. Allow repeated marking of the same angle, such as for laying out stair stringers. Attach them to the body and tongue of a carpenter's square.

Carpenter's level
Accurately indicates both level and plumb. Standard model is 24" long. Masons' levels are available up to 78" long; they are more accurate because the long body bridges surface contours. You can increase the accuracy of the standard level by placing it on a long, straight board. Electronic models are also available.

Carpenter's square
For laying out lines and checking square on large stock. Most durable squares are made from steel. Because accuracy depends on the square's exact shape, store it where it can't fall or be banged and bent by other tools.

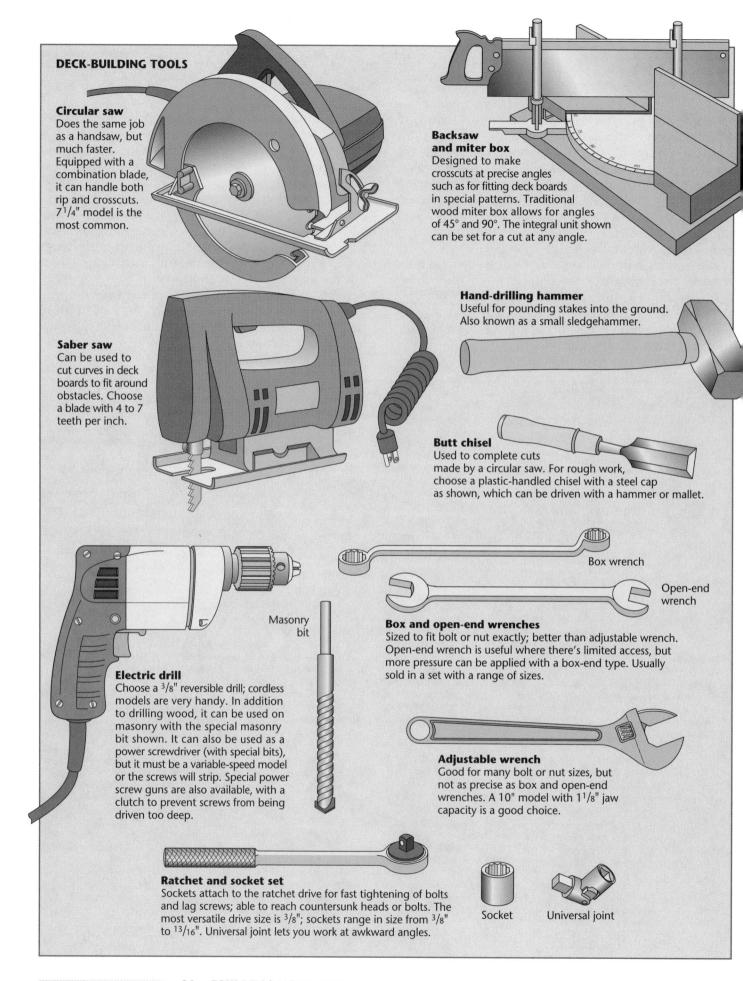

DECK-BUILDING TOOLS

Circular saw
Does the same job as a handsaw, but much faster. Equipped with a combination blade, it can handle both rip and crosscuts. $7^1/4$" model is the most common.

Saber saw
Can be used to cut curves in deck boards to fit around obstacles. Choose a blade with 4 to 7 teeth per inch.

Electric drill
Choose a $3/8$" reversible drill; cordless models are very handy. In addition to drilling wood, it can be used on masonry with the special masonry bit shown. It can also be used as a power screwdriver (with special bits), but it must be a variable-speed model or the screws will strip. Special power screw guns are also available, with a clutch to prevent screws from being driven too deep.

Backsaw and miter box
Designed to make crosscuts at precise angles such as for fitting deck boards in special patterns. Traditional wood miter box allows for angles of 45° and 90°. The integral unit shown can be set for a cut at any angle.

Hand-drilling hammer
Useful for pounding stakes into the ground. Also known as a small sledgehammer.

Butt chisel
Used to complete cuts made by a circular saw. For rough work, choose a plastic-handled chisel with a steel cap as shown, which can be driven with a hammer or mallet.

Masonry bit

Box wrench

Open-end wrench

Box and open-end wrenches
Sized to fit bolt or nut exactly; better than adjustable wrench. Open-end wrench is useful where there's limited access, but more pressure can be applied with a box-end type. Usually sold in a set with a range of sizes.

Adjustable wrench
Good for many bolt or nut sizes, but not as precise as box and open-end wrenches. A 10" model with $1^1/8$" jaw capacity is a good choice.

Ratchet and socket set
Sockets attach to the ratchet drive for fast tightening of bolts and lag screws; able to reach countersunk heads or bolts. The most versatile drive size is $3/8$"; sockets range in size from $3/8$" to $13/16$". Universal joint lets you work at awkward angles.

Socket

Universal joint

DECK STRUCTURE

Most decks share the same basic structure: Posts are anchored to a foundation of concrete footings and piers. The posts support beams, which in turn support joists. On an attached deck like the one shown below, a ledger fastened to the house takes the place of a beam, supporting one end of the joists. The deck is surfaced with deck boards ("decking") running across the joists. Raised decks require steps, and decks over 30 inches high also require a railing.

The structural members of a deck must be designed to support the necessary loads. The load they can support is determined by the spacing between them and their spans, as explained on the next page.

Although decks are built from the ground up, they are often designed from the top down, since the surface will be the most visible part. First decide how you want the deck surface to look, then design the substructure that will give it the support it requires.

DECK BASICS

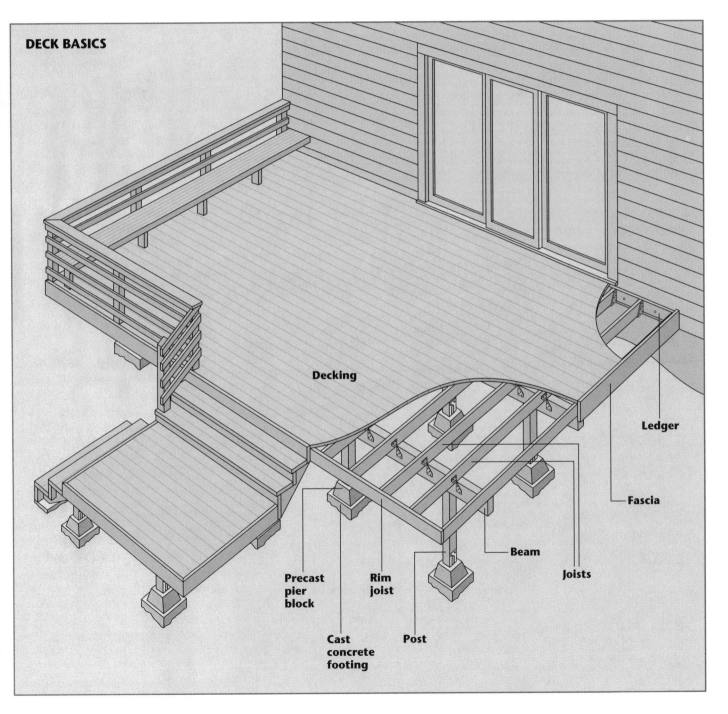

Decking

Ledger

Fascia

Beam

Joists

Precast pier block

Rim joist

Cast concrete footing

Post

CALCULATING SPANS

A deck's framework must be designed to withstand certain loads, as specified by the building code applicable to your area. Otherwise, under pressure from unusual stresses—a heavy snowfall or a large number of people at an outdoor party, for example—the structure may give way. The strength of the substructure is determined by the size and type of lumber used and by the spacing between structural members.

Loads: Though building codes vary, many areas require that a substructure be strong enough to support 40 pounds of live load (people, snow, etc.) plus 10 pounds of dead load (the weight of the construction materials themselves) per square foot (p.s.f). The tables and other design information given on the following pages are based on this "40 plus 10 p.s.f." loading at deck heights of up to 12 feet.

If your deck will be more than 8 feet above grade (even if only at one post), or if it must bear abnormally weighty loads, such as firewood or a very large planter, make sure to have your plans checked by an engineer; special reinforcement may be required.

Spans and spacings: As illustrated below, a span is the distance bridged by a deck board, joist, or beam;

spacing is the distance between adjacent joists, beams, or posts. Thus, the joist span is the same as the beam-to-beam spacing. Keep in mind that span refers to the distance the member spans from one support to the next, and not its total length.

Because they determine the ultimate strength or weakness of the support system, carefully figured spans and spacings are critical to proper substructure design.

As indicated in the following tables, the maximum safe spans and spacings for lumber of different dimensions depend on the species of wood and the grade you use.

ASK A PRO

CAN I PUT A SPA ON MY DECK?

Generally, a spa should be supported on its own structure, with the deck built around it—unless the spa manufacturer gives specific instructions on how to reinforce your deck to handle the added weight. It's best to check with your building department in either case.

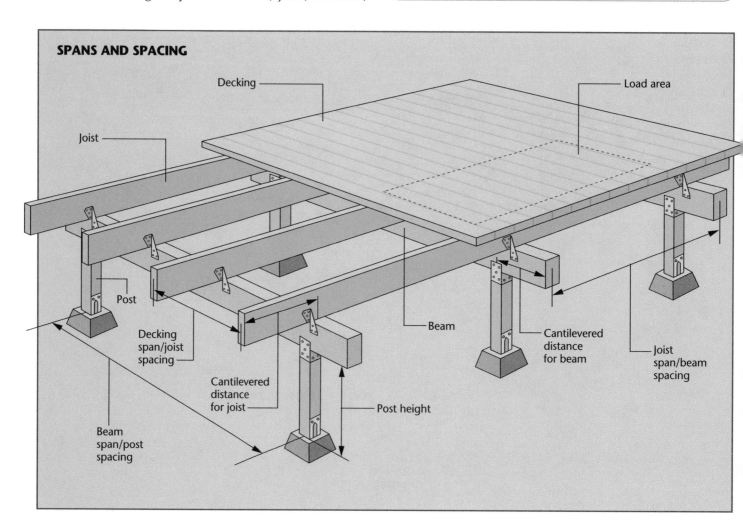

SPANS AND SPACING

Decking

Load area

Joist

Post

Decking span/joist spacing

Cantilevered distance for joist

Beam span/post spacing

Post height

Beam

Cantilevered distance for beam

Joist span/beam spacing

Cantilever: Joists that extend unsupported beyond the last beam are referred to as cantilevered. The unsupported part of the joist can be up to one-fourth of the span indicated in the span tables. For example, a joist that spans 12 feet between beams could be cantilevered 3 feet at each end. Thus, cantilevering joists is a way of increasing the size of the deck without adding another beam. These joists must be secured to the beams or ledger with metal framing anchors to avoid a seesaw effect when someone steps on the unsupported ends.

Similarly, beams can be cantilevered past the last post to one-fourth their post-to-post span. Deck boards should not be cantilevered more than a couple of inches.

USING SIZE, SPAN, AND SPACING TABLES

Use these five tables to calculate the proper sizes, spans, and heights for your deck's structural elements. The figures given are recommended maximums; you can choose shorter spans, closer spacings, or larger lumber for a more rigid structure. All lumber sizes are nominal. Spacings and spans are measured "on center," from the center of one member to the center of the next.

As you work through the tables, you'll see that any of several joist-beam-post combinations will work for a given situation. For example, as shown in Table 4, 4x8 beams spaced 10 feet apart may call for supporting posts every 6 feet; if spaced just 4 feet apart, the same beams would only require posts every 10 feet along their length. Some combinations may be more desirable than others because they require less lumber, easier-to-handle beams, or less foundation work.

The information in the tables conforms to the recommendations of the Council of American Building Officials (CABO). However, code requirements vary from one locale to another; they also change over time to adapt to changes in the composition of the wood supply. Use these tables for planning and design, but be sure to check with your building department as well.

TABLE 1: SOFTWOOD STRENGTH GROUPINGS
(Based on No. 2 and Better)

Group A	Douglas-fir, western hemlock, western larch, southern pine
Group B	Western cedar, Douglas-fir (South), hem/fir, alpine white fir, eastern mountain hemlock, pine (all but southern), redwood (Clear and Better), spruce (eastern, Engelmann, Sitka)
Group C	Redwood (Construction Common and Better)

Table 1—Softwood strength groupings: Lumber strength varies with species; this table groups species with comparable strength. Before using the span tables, check the strength grouping of your wood. The table assumes the use of No. 2 and Better grade lumber; pressure-treated wood falls into the same strength groupings as untreated wood of the same species and grade.

TABLE 2: DECKING SIZES AND SPANS
(On center measurements)

Maximum Spans for Species Group	A	B	C
1-by lumber laid flat	16"	14"	12"
Radius-edge decking	16"	16"	16"
2-by lumber laid flat	24"	24"	24"
2x3s laid on edge	48"	36"	32"
2x4s laid on edge	60"	60"	60"

Table 2—Decking spans: Now select the size of deck boards that you'll be installing. Then, using the strength group determined in Table 1, calculate the maximum distance your decking can span between joists—or between beams, if you plan to place on-edge boards directly on the beams. The table is applicable for any lumber of a grade appropriate for decking—grading systems vary depending on the type of wood (*page 20*). The spans indicated assume normal loads that are distributed evenly; if the loads will be concentrated, such as with a very large planter, the spans must be reduced. Greater spans are allowable with some decking materials, but be careful; this may result in an overly springy deck.

NOTE: For joists supporting diagonal boards, the allowed spacing in the table corresponds to the distance between the joists measured on the diagonal.

TABLE 3: MAXIMUM JOIST SPACINGS AND SPANS
(Maximum on center measurements based on No. 2 and Better joists placed on edge)

	Maximum Spans for Species Group		
	A	B	C
16" joist spacings			
2x6	9'9"	8'7"	7'9"
2x8	12'10"	11'4"	10'2"
2x10	16'5"	14'6"	13'
24" joist spacings			
2x6	8'6"	7'6"	6'9"
2x8	11'3"	9'11"	8'11"
2x10	14'4"	12'8"	11'4"
32" joist spacings			
2x6	7'9"	6'10"	6'2"
2x8	10'2"	9'	8'1"
2x10	13'	11'6"	10'4"

Table 3—Joist sizes and spans: Next, use this table to determine the correct size and beam-to-beam span of joists for the spacings determined in Table 2. You can start with either the joist size or joist span—the chart will provide the other one. The figures are based on joists placed on edge.

Remember that joists can be cantilevered up to one-fourth their span.

TABLE 4: BEAM SPACINGS AND SPANS

(Maximum on center measurements based on No. 2 and Better beams placed on edge)

Species Group	Beam Size	4'	5'	6'	7'	8'	9'	10'	11'	12'
A	4x6	6' spans →								
	3x8	8' →		7'	6' →					
	4x8	10'	9'	8'	7' →		6' →			
	3x10	11'	10'	9'	8'		7' →		6' →	
	4x10	12'	11'	10'	9' →		8' →		7' →	
	3x12		12'	11'	10'	9' →		8' →		
	4x12			12' →		11'	10' →		9' →	
	6x10						12'	11'	10' →	
B	4x6	6' →								
	3x8	7' →		6' →						
	4x8	9'	8'	7' →		6' →				
	3x10	10'	9'	8'	7' →		6' →			
	4x10	11'	10'	9'	8' →		7' →			6'
	3x12	12'	11'	10'	9'	8' →		7' →		
	4x12		12'	11'	10' →		9' →		8' →	
	6x10			12'	11'	10' →		9' →		
C	4x6	6'								
	3x8	7'	6'							
	4x8	8'	7'	6' →						
	3x10	9'	8'	7'	6' →					
	4x10	10'	9'	8' →		7' →		6' →		
	3x12	11'	10'	9'	8'	7' →			6' →	
	4x12	12'	11'	10'	9' →		8' →		7' →	
	6x10		12'	11'	10'	9' →		8' →		

ASK A PRO

HOW DO I DESIGN THE MOST COST-EFFECTIVE STRUCTURE?

If you're having the foundation built for you, you can minimize costs by using larger joists and beams, thus requiring fewer beams and less foundation work. (This will also save considerably on labor if you're constructing the foundation yourself.) To cut down on lumber used, take full advantage of cantilevering as described on page 41.

Table 4—Beam sizes and spans: Again, use the strength groupings to determine which size beams will span from post to post when set various distances apart. You may be limited by the beam sizes available. For this table, round the beam spacing down to the nearest whole foot before looking up the span.

If you're using a built-up beam of two 2-bys, you can use the spans indicated in the chart for a 3-by; however, this will mean using smaller spans or spacings than you really need. For more precise figures, consult an engineer.

Remember that beams can be cantilevered up to one-fourth their span.

Table 5—Minimum post sizes: To determine the post size, you'll need to know the wood grouping (Table 1), the joist span (Table 3), and the beam span (Table 4). Then, multiply the joist span (in feet) by the beam span (in feet) to determine the load area (in square feet) that each post supports—round up to the next largest load area listed. Finally, consult Table 5 to select a post size that meets the height requirements for your deck. In order to make construction simpler, try to use posts and beams of the same thickness.

If you'll be designing your deck with continuous posts to support an overhead, consult a professional for the best size of post for the height and load.

TABLE 5: MINIMUM POST SIZES

(Maximum on center measurements based on Standard and Better for 4x4 posts, No. 1 and Better for larger sizes.)

Species Group	Post Size	36	48	60	72	84	96	108	120	132	144
A	4x4	12' high →				10' high →		8' high →			
	4x6					12' →			10' →		
	6x6								12' →		
B	4x4	12' →	10' →			8' →					
	4x6			12' →		10' →					
	6x6				12' →						
C	4x4	12'	10' →	8' →		6' →					
	4x6		12' →		10' →		8' →				
	6x6				12' →						

LEDGERS

A ledger is a board fastened to a house wall or other structure to support one end of the joists. Installing the ledger is generally the first step in building an attached deck because it will be used as a reference point to lay out the rest of the deck. Locate the ledger so the surface of the deck will be one inch below the door; this will help keep out rain and snow. You'll have to take into account the thickness of the decking, and if the joists will rest on the ledger, the height of the joists.

Ledgers on low decks, up to 3 feet high, are usually made of 2x6 or 2x8 lumber, typically the same size or one size bigger than the joists. Taller decks require more support and the ledger should be made of 4-by lumber. Be sure to use pressure-treated lumber if the ledger will be close to the ground or fastened to masonry.

Ledgers must be solidly attached to either the house framing or a masonry wall. In the case of wood framing, the ledger should be attached to either the band joist or the blocking between floor joists, as shown below. If the ledger falls between the floors of the house it can be attached to wall studs. In all cases, use either lag screws or through bolts—nails are never sufficient.

A ledger can be attached to a solid brick wall or a concrete foundation wall using masonry anchors. However, if your brick wall is crumbling or the bricks are loose,

you'd be well-advised to opt for a freestanding deck rather than trying to fasten a ledger to the brick. Neither stucco nor a thin brick facade offers enough support—you should fasten right through these materials into the framing.

Water will tend to collect between the ledger and the house wall, which can be problematic if you have a wood frame house. To prevent water from collecting, there are two options: You can either space the ledger out from the wall with washers as shown below, or cover the joint with flashing as shown in the inset—instructions for installing flashing are given on page 45. (NOTE: Washers should not be used with a stucco wall because they will tend to sink into the wall surface.)

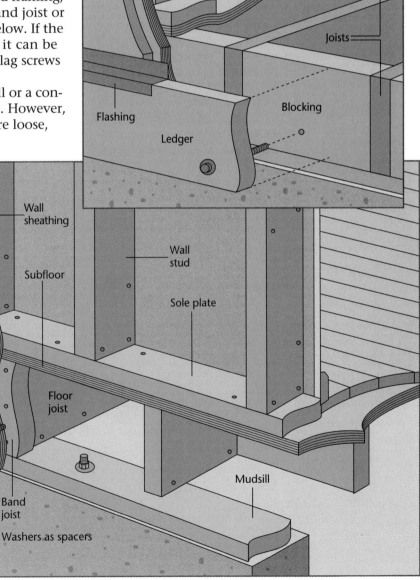

Flashing

Joists

Blocking

Ledger

Door

Siding

Wall sheathing

Subfloor

Wall stud

Sole plate

Floor joist

Ledger

Allowance for thickness of decking and slight drop

Foundation wall

Bolt or lag screw

Band joist

Washers as spacers

Mudsill

SHOULD I REMOVE THE SIDING TO INSTALL A LEDGER?

Siding should be removed if it's a type that doesn't rest flat against the house sheathing or framing. An example would be the clapboard siding shown near right. The pressure of the ledger will crush the siding, resulting in a less solid and attractive joint. Wood shingle, vinyl, and aluminum siding should also be removed.

If the siding rests flat against the sheathing, as in the case of the rabbeted-bevel siding shown at far right, it can be left in place. If the outside surface of the siding is not smooth, add a shim as shown to provide a smooth surface for the ledger; the shim can be made of a piece of siding turned upside down.

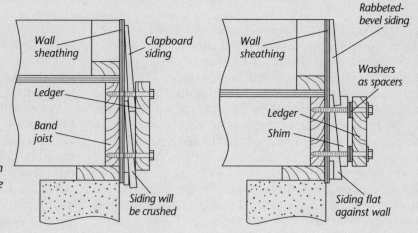

To remove siding, use a circular saw, finishing the cuts with a butt chisel. For making vertical cuts, you'll need to bridge the uneven surface of overlapping siding: Rest the saw's base on a 1-by board attached to the wall. Remove enough siding so that there is about a 1-inch gap between the bottom of the siding and the top of the ledger.

Attaching a ledger

TOOLKIT
- Tape measure
- Carpenter's level
- Water level and chalk line (optional)
- Claw hammer
- Electric drill
- Socket wrench
For wood framing:
- Hand-drilling hammer for stakes
- Caulking gun

Fastening a ledger to wood framing

First, mark a level line indicating the top of the ledger. Use a long level, or mark two points with a water level and join them with a chalk line. Brace or nail the ledger in place as shown. Then, if you can access the inside of the house framing to add washers and nuts, drill all the way through the framing and fasten the ledger with 1/2" carriage bolts—one at each end of the ledger and staggered up and down every 16" (you'll have to position the bolts so they come out between the floor joists). If the inside framing isn't accessible, use 1/2" lag screws. To install lag screws, first drill clearance holes through the ledger and then a pilot hole into the framing.

Remove the ledger and pack each pilot hole with silicone caulk for moisture protection. Run lag screws into the ledger until the points protrude about 1/2". (The screws should penetrate the framing at least 1 1/2", or as specified by local codes.) If you're not planning to use flashing, slip several large washers onto each lag screw, to leave a space of about 3/8" between the house wall and ledger. Working with a helper, line up the lag screws with the holes and tighten them using a socket wrench.

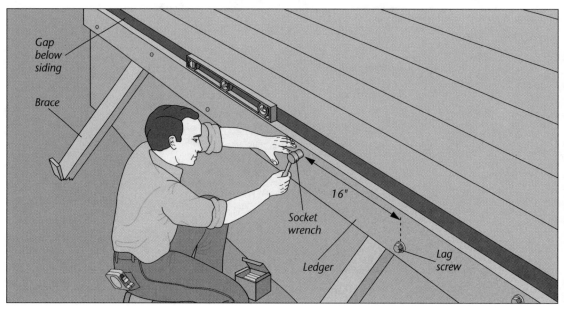

Fastening a ledger to a masonry wall or foundation

Mark the location of the top of the ledger as described for wood framing. Drill holes for expanding anchor bolts, staggering them every 16" as shown.

Tap in the anchor bolts with a hammer. Then, working with a helper, hold the ledger in place, making sure it's level, and tap it with a hammer to indent the bolt locations on it. Remove the ledger and drill holes through it at the marks made by the bolt tips. Or, you can measure and transfer the bolt locations to the ledger.

Push (or hammer) the ledger onto the bolts; add washers and nuts, and tighten.

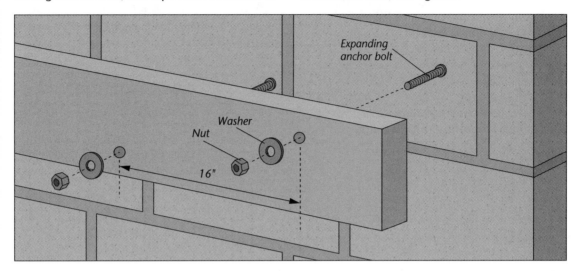

Flashing the ledger

TOOLKIT
- Tin snips
- Prybar for siding or shingles (optional)
- Caulking gun
- Circular saw with masonry blade for stucco

Installing the flashing

For a wood frame house, you'll have to keep moisture from penetrating the space between the ledger and the house wall. If you haven't spaced the ledger out with washers, you'll need to flash the joint. This should be done before you fasten the joists in place. You can use either aluminum or galvanized sheet metal Z-flashing. Cut the flashing to length with tin snips.

If the wall is finished with wood siding or shingles, slip the flashing up under the edge of the siding and then pull it down to rest on the top of the ledger (below, left). You may need to pry up the siding a bit to get the flashing in. You don't have to fasten the flashing—the siding will hold it in place. If you've removed a section of siding, caulk the ends of the flashing where they butt up against the adjoining siding. Use silicone rubber sealant.

For a stucco wall, use flashing with a crimped top edge (you'll have to have it made at a sheet metal shop). Cut a groove in the siding with a circular saw equipped with a masonry blade. Fit the crimped edge of the flashing into the groove (below, right). Caulk the edge of the flashing where it enters the groove.

It's important to caulk any end joints between adjacent pieces of flashing as well as the edge where the flashing butts up against the bottom of the door threshold.

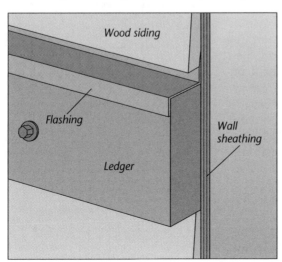

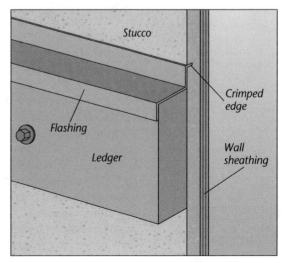

FOUNDATION

Your deck must rest on a solid foundation of concrete footings and piers. The locations of the footings must be carefully laid out, as explained below. The next step is to dig the holes, and then you'll be ready to mix and cast the concrete.

Casting concrete can be heavy work—you may want to consider hiring experienced workers for this part of the job, especially if you're building a large deck with many footings. If you're going to do the work yourself, make sure you have help.

ASK A PRO

WHAT DO I HAVE TO DO TO PREPARE MY SITE FOR A DECK?

Before building a deck, take care of any grading or drainage problems on your lot, since the area will be inaccessible once the deck is in place. Your lot should slope away from the house, about 1 inch for every 10 feet. If you find standing water after rain, you may have a drainage problem—consult a professional on where to redirect the water. You may also have to knock down high spots that might interfere with the deck.

Consider taking steps to prevent weed growth under your deck. Many commercial weed killers are harmful for the environment and hazardous for small children and pets; instead, you can cover the ground with black polyethylene sheeting or landscape fabric. Weight down the sheeting or fabric with bricks, stones, or gravel; poke drainage holes in plastic sheeting.

LAYOUT

The placement of footings of course depends on where the deck posts will be placed. And post locations in turn are determined by beam and joist spans. Use the span tables on pages 41 and 42 to work out all these measurements, then transfer the footing locations to the ground, as shown beginning with the illustration below.

The ledger will be used as a reference point to locate the footings, but you'll have to ensure that all the corners of the deck are perfectly square. To do this, you can use the 3-4-5 method, as described below. If you lay out a triangle with these dimensions (or any multiple, such as 6-8-10) the corner will be exactly 90°. Using the largest possible multiple will ensure maximum accuracy.

Locating the footings

TOOLKIT
• Claw hammer
• Tape measure
• Hand-drilling hammer for driving in batterboards (optional)
• Carpenter's square
• Carpenter's level
• Plumb bob

1 ▶ Setting up string lines perpendicular to the house

Hammer a nail into the top of the ledger board at a point in line with the center of the corner post, and then set up a batterboard about 18" past the location of this post. Stretch a string from the ledger to the batterboard, using a carpenter's square to check that it is about 90° to the ledger.

To check for exact square, measure 6' along the ledger and mark the point. Then put a mark on the string with a piece of colored tape 8' away from the ledger. Move the string back and forth along the batterboard until the diagonal is exactly 10', as shown at right; hammer a nail into the top of the batterboard at the spot you've established. Leave the nail sticking out a couple of inches, and attach the string to it. Repeat this procedure at the other end of the deck to set up a second string line.

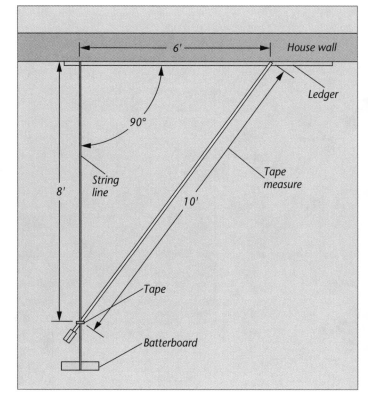

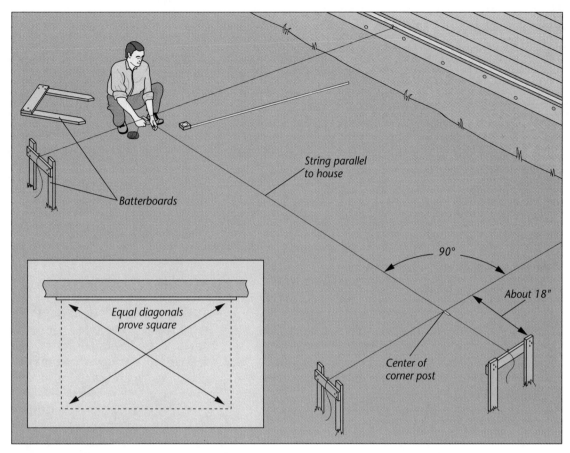

Batterboards

String parallel
to house

90°

About 18"

Center of
corner post

Equal diagonals
prove square

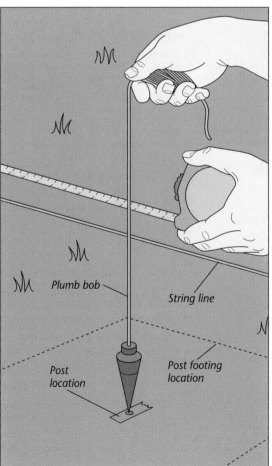

Plumb bob

String line

Post
location

Post footing
location

2 Setting up a string line parallel to the house

Measure away from the house along each string line and use colored tape to mark a point corresponding to the center of each corner post; make sure the tape measure is level. Set up two more batterboards near the tape on the strings and stretch another string between them, parallel to the ledger board and crossing the original strings at the tape *(above)*. (Make sure to keep the batterboards about 18" away from the post locations so they don't get in the way when you're digging.) You should now have a complete rectangle formed of string lines and the house wall.

The point where the strings cross indicates the center of each corner post. To make sure everything is exactly square, measure both diagonals and adjust the strings until the diagonal distances are identical *(inset)*.

3 Marking post locations

Use a plumb bob to transfer the point where the strings cross down to the ground; mark the point with a small flag (drive a large nail through a piece of colored tape), a stake, or lime. Then, measure along the strings and plumb down to mark all the other post locations as shown; make sure your tape measure is level.

WORKING WITH CONCRETE

You'll have to mix, transport, and cast a fair amount of concrete to build your deck's foundation. Plan for some heavy work that may be quite time-consuming, depending on the number of footings you require.

You'll need a large container to mix your concrete. Mortar boxes can be purchased, but you can substitute a large plastic bin, a wheelbarrow, or even a sheet of plywood. You'll want a square shovel to measure the concrete ingredients. The best tool for the actual mixing is a mortar hoe, but you can use a shovel instead. A mason's trowel, or other small trowel, is needed to test the consistency of your concrete mixture.

BUYING CONCRETE

How you buy your concrete will depend on the size of your project and how much time and energy you have. You can choose among the following options:

Bulk dry ingredients: If your project is large, you can save money by mixing your own concrete from dry ingredients—a formula is given below. You'll find that this method is even more economical if you haul the materials yourself.

Dry prepackaged mix: This is by far the most convenient option for a small job. The dry ingredients come premixed and require only the addition of water.

Haul-it-yourself mix: Some dealers provide trailers you can haul with your car. These trailers contain about 1 cubic yard of concrete with the water already added. They may have a revolving drum that mixes the concrete as you go. CAUTION: Be sure the tires and brakes on your vehicle are in good condition and that both your vehicle and trailer hitch are capable of taking the weight.

Ready-mix: Commercial ready-mix trucks can deliver a large quantity all at once. This is the best choice for a very large job. NOTE: Many concrete suppliers require that you buy a certain minimum amount.

MIXING AND CASTING CONCRETE

For a small project, the simplest method is to mix the concrete by hand. For jobs that require casting 3 cubic feet or more at once, you may want to rent an electric mixer. Instructions for both methods are given on the next page.

Mix the concrete according to the formula given at left. Each footing must be cast at once—one batch of concrete should not be allowed to dry before the next one is placed. So, for large footings, you'll probably want to have one person mixing while other people push the loaded wheelbarrows and place the concrete. If you're working with a ready-mix truck, you'll need extra hands to move the concrete from the truck to the site.

A CONCRETE FORMULA

All proportions are by volume. The sand should be clean concrete sand (never beach sand); the aggregate should range in size from quite small to about $3/4$ inch in size. The water should be drinkable—neither excessively alkaline nor acidic, nor containing organic matter. The following is a good formula to use for concrete footings:

    1 part portland cement
    $2^1/_2$ parts sand
    $2^1/_2$ parts stone or gravel aggregate
    $1/_2$ part water

To know how much concrete to buy, refer to the table below. The figures given are for 10 cubic feet of finished concrete and include 10% extra for waste. Note that the final volume is less than the sum of the ingredients because the smaller particles fit in among the larger ones. If you order bulk materials sold by the cubic yard, remember that each cubic yard contains 27 cubic feet.

INGREDIENTS FOR 10 CUBIC FEET OF CONCRETE	
Bulk dry materials	Portland cement: 2.6 sacks Sand: 5.8 sacks Aggregate: 6.5 cubic feet
Dry prepackaged mix	20 60-pound bags
Ready-mix	.41 cubic yards

 ASK A PRO

HOW CAN I TELL IF MY CONCRETE IS THE RIGHT CONSISTENCY?

When mixing your own concrete, start by making a trial batch. Work a sample of this batch with a trowel: The concrete should slide off the trowel, but not run freely. You should be able to smooth the surface of the concrete with your trowel so that the large pieces of aggregate are submerged. All the aggregate at the edges of the sample should be evenly coated with cement. If your mix is too stiff and crumbly, add a little water. If it's too wet and soupy, add some cement-sand mixture, in the proportions required by your recipe.

Once you've made the adjustments necessary to achieve the right consistency, record how much extra water or cement-sand mix you've added and maintain these proportions for the other batches.

Mixing concrete

Using a mortar hoe

To mix by hand, you can put the materials in a wheelbarrow or mortar box—for small batches—or on a piece of plywood—for large batches—and use a mortar hoe or shovel as your mixing tool. To measure out the ingredients, use shovelfuls for the dry ingredients. Use a pail for the water after finding out how many shovelfuls it takes to fill your pail.

First, spread the sand and cement on the mixing surface. Using a rolling motion, mix these ingredients until the color is even. Add the aggregate; again, mix until the color is even. Finally, scoop out a hole in the middle of the dry ingredients and add the water.

Work around the edges of the puddle with the hoe or shovel, slowly rolling the dry ingredients into the water. Take particular care not to slop the water out of the wheelbarrow (or off the platform), since escaping water may weaken the batch by carrying particles of cement with it.

Work in small batches to make mixing easier and keep control over proportions.

Using a concrete mixer

Set up the mixer close to your supplies of sand and aggregate so you can feed the machine directly from the piles. Measure out the ingredients as described above. Wedge the machine firmly in place and make sure that it is level.

First, with the mixer off, add the coarse aggregate and half the water. Then, turn on the machine to scour the drum. (If the machine is gas-powered, you'll need to warm it up.) Next, add the sand, and all but about 10% of the water. Then, add the portland cement. When the mixture is an even color and consistency, add the rest of the water. Mix for at least two minutes or until the mixture has reached a uniform appearance. Measure the dry ingredients by equal shovelfuls as you add them; never put the shovel inside the mixer while it's in operation.

PLAY IT SAFE

WORKING WITH A CONCRETE MIXER

Be sure to follow all safety measures for the mixer you're using. Never reach into the rotating drum with either your hands or tools. Wear tight-fitting clothes, a dust mask, and goggles, and keep away from the moving parts. Do not look into the mixer while it's running—check the mix by dumping some out.

An electric mixer must be plugged into a ground fault circuit interrupter (GFCI) outlet and should have a three-prong grounding-type plug; use only an outdoor-rated three-prong extension cord. Don't run an electric mixer in damp conditions, and cover it with a tarpaulin when not in use.

To fuel a gasoline-powered mixer, use the proper type of can for storing and pouring flammable fuel. Add fuel only when the engine is off and has cooled down; close the fuel container tightly after fueling. Wipe up any fuel spills immediately. Don't stand where you must breathe the exhaust fumes and never run the mixer in an enclosed space.

CASTING THE FOUNDATION

Your deck's foundation anchors the entire structure against settling, slippage, and wind lift; it distributes loads into the ground, and protects posts or beams from direct contact with the earth. The foundation generally consists of two parts, a footing that distributes the load underground and a pier that raises the bottom of the post above grade, as shown on the next page.

The size and depth of footings are governed by code. Typical footings are 18 inches square and extend 6 inches below the frost line.

Piers can be cylindrical, rectangular, or pyramidal with a flat top; the top surface should be large enough for a post anchor. The pier should hold the bottom of the post 6 inches above grade to protect it from decay; this is essential with an untreated post and is recommended even for treated posts. If you're using an untreated post, choose a raised post anchor, such as one of the ones shown on page 26, that provides an inch of clearance between the concrete and the bottom of the post. Whatever type of post you choose, you can increase its life by placing an asphalt shingle between the post anchor and the bottom of the post.

On page 51 we explain three methods for constructing a foundation. The simplest is to cast the footing and then place a precast pier on it. A selection of precast piers is shown on page 50—for maximum hold-down strength choose the type with either a metal post anchor or a metal strap. Alternatively, you can cast both the

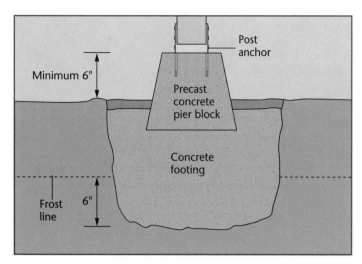

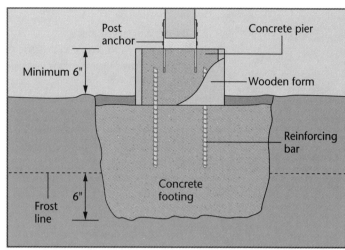

footing and the pier yourself; this will allow you a greater selection of post anchors. The third method is to use fiber tubes to cast a cylindrical column. This is a good choice in areas with a very deep frost line, because it makes it easy to extend the footing up to the surface.

An alternative to footings and piers is to cast the end of a pressure-treated post directly in the footing. This method offers some additional lateral stability, but even a treated post will rot eventually when in contact with concrete, and any future repairs will be difficult to perform.

When casting concrete footings and piers, you may need to add steel bars for reinforcement. Requirements for these steel reinforcements are governed by local building codes.

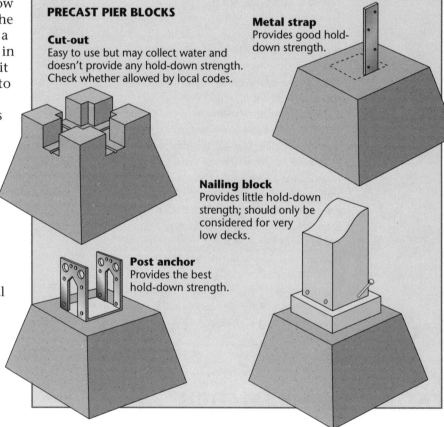

PRECAST PIER BLOCKS

Cut-out
Easy to use but may collect water and doesn't provide any hold-down strength. Check whether allowed by local codes.

Metal strap
Provides good hold-down strength.

Nailing block
Provides little hold-down strength; should only be considered for very low decks.

Post anchor
Provides the best hold-down strength.

Digging footing holes

TOOLKIT
- Pointed shovel
- Hand auger, post-hole digger, or power auger (optional)

Choosing the right tool

Footings up to about 2' deep are best dug with a pointed shovel. For deeper holes, you'll want a more specialized tool to dig the holes and remove the earth. Hand augers use a twisting motion to collect the earth; they are best used in loose soil. For hard or rocky soil, choose a post-hole digger with a pair of blades operated with handles (these are difficult to use for holes deeper than 3'). If you have more than about a dozen holes to dig, it might be worth renting a power auger. In general, footings must be cast on solid, undisturbed soil; if you dig too deep, just cast the footing deeper rather than filling the earth back in (soil that has been backfilled will tend to settle). In some areas, gravel is recommended below the footing for drainage—check your building code.

NOTE: You'll have to remove the string lines to dig the footing holes and cast the concrete; replace them afterwards in order to line up the pier blocks or post anchors.

Casting footings and adding piers

TOOLKIT
- Mortar hoe or shovel for placing concrete
- Carpenter's level

For wooden forms:
- Claw hammer or screwdriver

For fiber form tubes:
- Crosscut saw
- Hand-drilling hammer
- Claw hammer

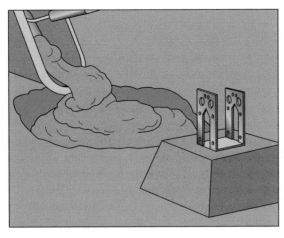

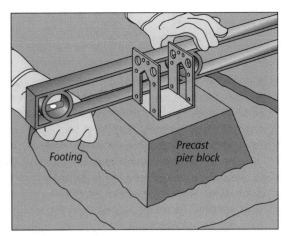

Footing · Precast pier block

Using precast pier blocks
First soak the pier blocks with a hose. Then, cast the footings to the depth and size required by the local building code *(above, left)*; the top of the footing should be about 1" below grade. Wait a few minutes—until the concrete has stiffened enough to support the piers—then position the pier blocks and level them in both directions *(above, right)*; align the post anchors with the string lines. Cover the exposed part of the footings with earth to prevent the concrete from drying too quickly.

Using wooden forms
Use plywood or scrap lumber for forms. If you'll be casting several piers over a period of weeks, hinge the forms so they can be opened and reused. Otherwise, use duplex nails for easy disassembly. Reinforce large forms with wire.

First, cast all the footings to the depth and size required by local codes; their tops should be about 1" below grade. Wait a few minutes, then set and level the piers' forms over the wet concrete footings, inserting steel reinforcing rods, if required, to strengthen the link between the footings and the piers. Fill the pier forms with concrete; use a straight board to level the concrete flush with the tops of the forms. Immediately embed a metal post anchor *(page 26)* in each wet concrete pier,

aligning it with the string lines. Before the concrete begins to stiffen, check for plumb: Hold a carpenter's level against two adjacent sides of a short length of post material placed in the post anchor. Use your string line to make sure the anchor is in line with or at right angles to the direction the beam will run. Make any necessary adjustments.

After the concrete has begun to set, cover the top of the footings with earth to keep them damp while the concrete cures. Leave the forms on the new piers while the concrete cures, and to protect them from direct sun or hot, dry weather, cover with newspapers, straw, or burlap sacks. Keep the covering moist for at least a week so the piers will dry slowly.

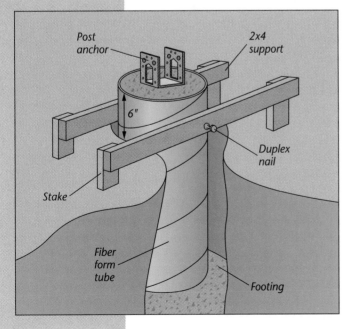

Post anchor · 2x4 support · 6" · Duplex nail · Stake · Fiber form tube · Footing

Using fiber form tubes
The hole for the fiber form tube must be splayed at the bottom to allow the concrete to spread out to form a footing. Cut the tube to length and suspend it; it should be about 6" above the bottom of the hole and extend at least 6" above grade. Hold the tube at the right height by nailing a staked 2x4 laid on edge to each side of the tube using duplex nails as shown. For taller columns, also brace the tubes as you would brace a post *(page 55)*.

Insert steel rods if necessary and place the concrete. Smooth off the top with a piece of wood and immediately insert a metal post anchor; align it using the string lines. Make sure the anchor is level by inserting a piece of post material in the anchor and checking it for plumb with a carpenter's level.

Fill in the hole around the tube with earth. Cover the top of the tube with newspaper, straw, or burlap and keep it damp for at least a week. Then peel off the part of the tube that sticks up above the ground.

If you have a damaged or unsightly patio, the easiest and least expensive way to update it may be to cover it with a new deck. Sleepers made of pressure-treated 2x3s or 2x4s will take the place of joists; they'll be fastened directly to the slab and spaced the same distance apart as joists. If your patio has low spots, you'll have to shim the sleepers with small redwood wedges or cedar shingles; space these approximately every 24 inches.

You can fasten the sleepers to the slab with adhesive, expanding anchor bolts, or angle irons. Another alternative is to fasten the sleepers by "shooting" them down with a powder-actuated tool. These tools can be rented or purchased; they use a blank cartridge with gun powder as an energy source, and special training is required to operate them. Be sure to follow all safety directions provided with the tool.

Once the sleepers are in place, you can install the decking in the usual way *(page 69)*. If you wish, you can add a fascia to cover the edges of the decking.

If you want the deck to extend past the edge of the old patio, use 4x4s as sleepers and support the ends that are beyond the patio with a typical arrangement of footings and piers. You may have to partially bury the piers for their top surface to arrive at the right level. NOTE: A powder-actuated tool cannot be used to fasten 4x4s.

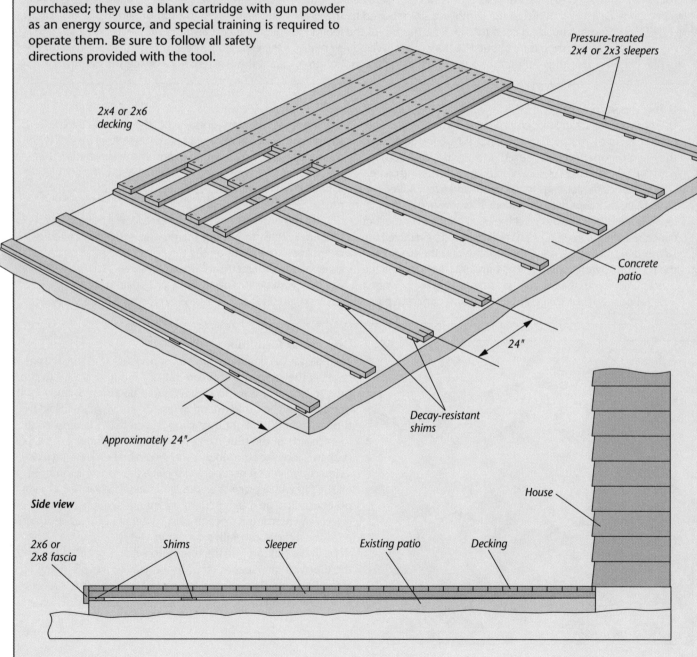

Pressure-treated
2x4 or 2x3 sleepers

2x4 or 2x6
decking

Concrete
patio

24"

Decay-resistant
shims

Approximately 24"

House

Side view

2x6 or
2x8 fascia

Shims

Sleeper

Existing patio

Decking

POSTS AND BEAMS

Deck posts are connected to the piers with post anchors. Beams usually sit on top of the posts, connected to them with post caps (for a selection turn to page 25). Alternatively, the beams can mesh with the posts as in the sandwiched post or beam designs shown below. These arrangements allow the posts to extend upwards above the surface of the deck, the sturdiest way to support railings, screens, overheads, and benches. NOTE: For the sandwiched beam design, you'll have to insert a 4-by block into the post anchor and fasten the 2-by lumber to it.

MATERIALS

Although most deck posts are made of 4x4s, various other materials can be used: larger sizes of dimension lumber, built-up lumber, steel, or a combination of these. (For more information on post materials, turn to page 17.)

Beams may be solid lumber—commonly 4x6s or 4x8s—or built up from lengths of 2-by lumber fastened together as shown on page 56. Large beams are usually easiest to handle if they're built up, since they can be carried to their final destination in pieces. However, a single, solid beam is generally favored for a highly visible location.

INSTALLATION

You can begin to erect posts and beams once the concrete footings have cured for at least a week. The directions given starting on page 55 assume a simple construction method with beams sitting on top of the posts. For a stable, level substructure, posts must be measured accurately and cut squarely. If your deck is attached to the house, start by measuring the posts farthest from the house, using the ledger as a reference point. For a freestanding deck, begin by marking the posts along one edge, using these as a reference point for marking the posts along the opposite edge. Finally, mark any intermediate posts.

NOTE: Treat all saw cuts and drilled holes in pressure-treated wood with a brush-on wood preservative such as copper naphthanate.

PLAY IT SAFE

WORKING WITH PRESSURE-TREATED WOOD
Wood can be preserved with a number of different chemicals; the wood you find at a lumberyard has most likely been treated with inorganic arsenicals. This wood should never be burned. Dispose of it by burying it or by including it with your ordinary trash collection.

When cutting this type of lumber, always wear respiratory protection (a dust mask or respirator) and safety goggles. Wash your hands before eating and launder work clothes separately from other clothing.

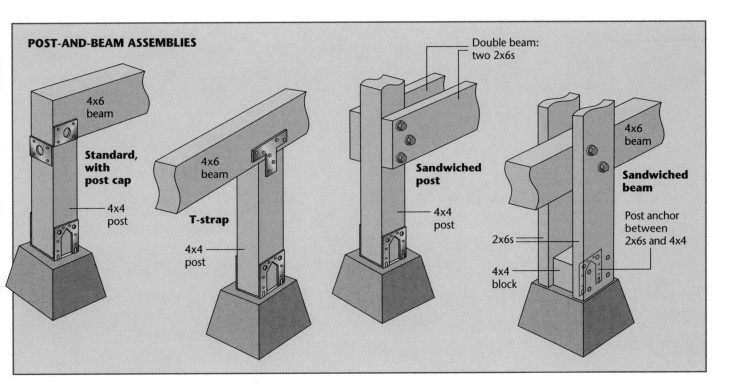

POST-AND-BEAM ASSEMBLIES

4x6 beam

Standard, with post cap

4x4 post

Double beam: two 2x6s

4x6 beam

T-strap

4x4 post

Sandwiched post

4x4 post

4x6 beam

Sandwiched beam

Post anchor between 2x6s and 4x4

2x6s

4x4 block

BRACING

Tall posts must be braced in order to ensure lateral stability. To determine the need for bracing, you must consult your local building codes, but in general, you can count on bracing in the following situations:

•All posts of freestanding decks over 36 inches high;

•Perimeter posts of attached decks over 36 inches high;

•All posts of attached decks taller than 8 feet;

•All posts of attached decks (regardless of their height) projecting farther than 20 feet from the house, or for decks projecting for more than twice the length of the attached side;

•All posts of decks exposed to high winds, earthquakes, or big loads.

You can choose from the bracing styles shown below. Plan to use 2x4s for distances less than 8 feet, and 2x6s for greater distances. To protect the bracing from decay, always cut the pieces so that the end grain will be vertical, as in the examples shown—horizontal end grain will absorb water. When using Y-bracing, a 90° angle between the pieces of bracing gives the strongest support.

Instructions for installing bracing are given on page 57. If you'd rather avoid this entire procedure, a structural engineer may be able to modify the design of your deck's substructure to eliminate the need for bracing.

NOTE: If installing a decorative skirt around the posts, choose a type of bracing that won't interfere with it.

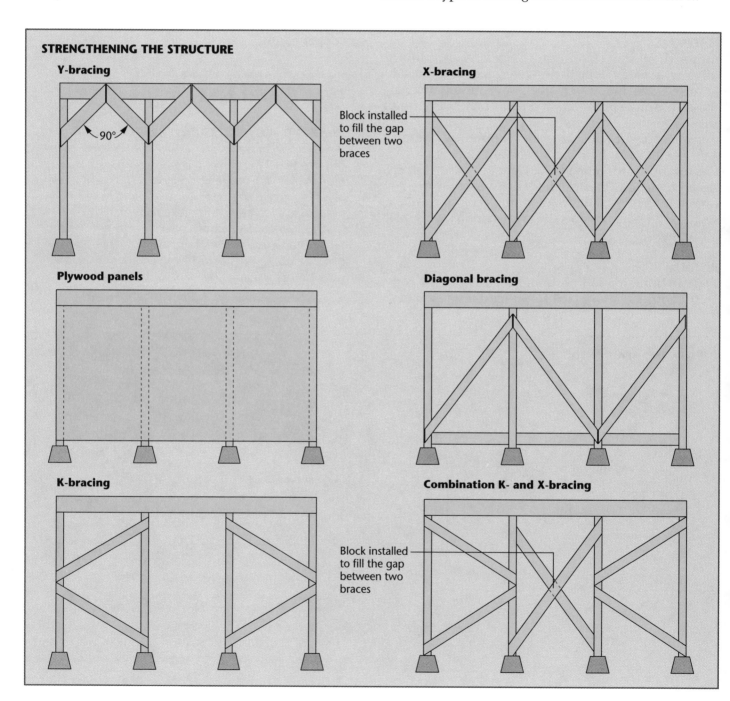

STRENGTHENING THE STRUCTURE

Y-bracing

90°

X-bracing

Block installed to fill the gap between two braces

Plywood panels

Diagonal bracing

K-bracing

Combination K- and X-bracing

Block installed to fill the gap between two braces

Installing posts

TOOLKIT
- Tape measure
- Combination square
- Circular saw
- Crosscut saw
- Carpenter's level
- Line level or water level
- Claw hammer
- Electric drill and wrenches if using bolts
- Hand-drilling hammer for driving stakes (optional)

1 Marking the posts

First cut a post 6" to 12" longer than the estimated finished length, using a circular saw (you may need to finish the cut with a crosscut saw). Have a helper hold the post firmly in place on its anchor; then plumb it, using a carpenter's level—check two adjacent sides. Use a line level *(page 37)* or a water level to mark the post at the same height as the bottom of the joists; this will usually be at the bottom of the ledger, but if you're using a ledger that is wider than the joists, you'll need to measure down from the top of the ledger to determine where the bottom of the joists will fall.

To use a water level, make sure the tube is free of air bubbles. Tape one end of the tube to the ledger and adjust the other end against the post until the level of the water at the taped end is at the right height *(below, left)*. The water at the post will be at the same level—mark this point on the post. Repeat for all the posts.

If the joists will sit on top of the beams, measure down the actual height of the beam from your first mark. Using a combination square, mark this new height on all four sides of the post *(below)*.

If the joists will butt against the beam, extend the first mark on all sides of the post. if the beam is wider than the joist, first move the mark down to where the bottom of the beam will fall.

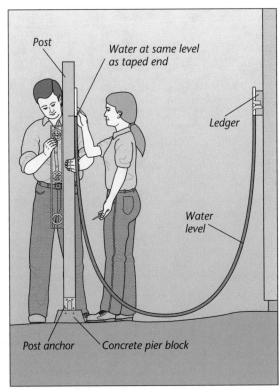

Post / Water at same level as taped end / Ledger / Water level / Post anchor / Concrete pier block

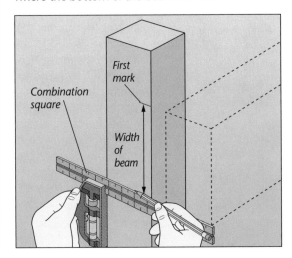

Combination square / First mark / Width of beam

2 Cutting and setting the posts

Take down each post and cut it on your marks. If you're using pressure-treated wood, treat the cut end with brush-on preservative. Fasten a post cap to the top of each post.

Before moving the first post into position, drive stakes into the ground to hold two braces on adjacent sides of the post. Use 1x2s or 1x3s for the braces, and position the stakes so that the braces will reach midway up the post at a 45° angle (be sure you cut the braces long enough). Nail the braces to each stake; to allow the brace to pivot, use only one nail.

Seat the post squarely in its anchor; if you're using a pressure-treated post, place the uncut end down to take maximum advantage of the pressure treatment. Check for plumb, using a carpenter's level on two adjacent sides. Nail the braces to the post, keeping the post plumb. Then nail or bolt the post to its anchor. Finally, drive additional nails into each brace to secure the posts until the beams are seated.

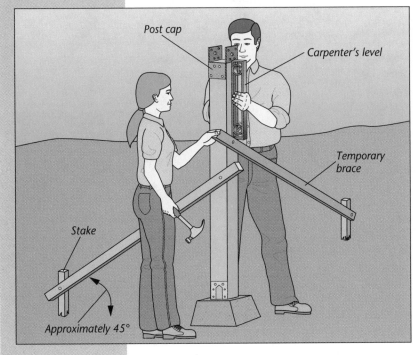

Post cap / Carpenter's level / Temporary brace / Stake / Approximately 45°

HOW CAN I MAKE A BUILT-UP BEAM?

A typical built-up beam consists of 2-by lumber nailed together with $1/2$-inch pressure-treated plywood spacers in between. The total thickness of the beam will work out to $3^1/_2$ inches—the same as the actual size of a 4-by post. Place the spacers 24 inches apart on center and nail the beam together with four nails through each spacer from each side as shown. The spacers should be pointed at the top to prevent water from collecting.

If you must make a long beam from shorter lengths, stagger the end joints; each joint should fall over a post. Sight along each piece to find the crown. Align the crowns on the same side; when you install the beam, it should go crown side up.

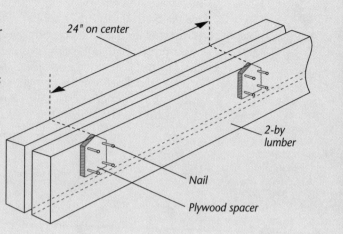

24" on center

2-by lumber

Nail

Plywood spacer

Installing beams

TOOLKIT
- Claw hammer if using nails

OR
- Electric drill and wrenches if using bolts

Seating a beam

Beams that sit directly on piers are nailed or bolted to the metal post anchors. Beams seated on low posts can be lifted into position easily, but raising heavy beams onto fairly tall posts is another story.

Before seating a beam, sight down it to find the crown, if any. When you mount the beam on the posts, place it crown side up unless the beam is cantilevered at one or both ends, in which case the crown side should face down.

To seat a heavy beam, drag it beside the posts, then slip a short length of 2x4 under one of its ends. With a helper, lift the 2x4 to raise that end of the beam into the post cap *(right)*. Temporarily nail the beam with one nail through one of the top holes in the post cap, then lift and place the other end. (With four people, you can lift both ends of the beam into position at once.) This is heavy work—be sure of your footing, and always wear a hard hat.

Nail the beam to the post cap. If you're using bolts, mark the bolt positions through the holes in the anchor; then, lift the beam out of the cap and set it on a piece of wood on top of the cap. Drill from one side of the beam until the drill tip shows on the other side; then finish the hole from the other direction. Treat the bolt holes with brush-on preservative and lastly, bolt the beam to the post cap.

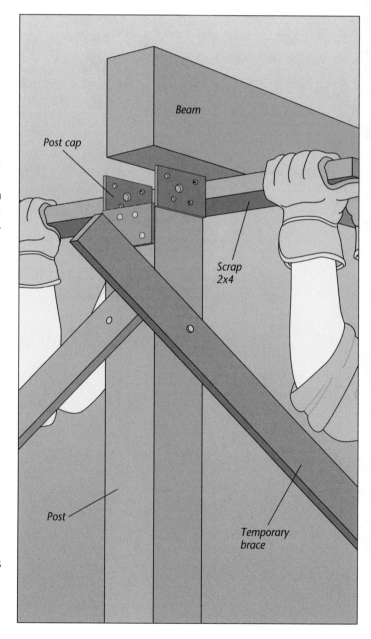

Beam

Post cap

Scrap 2x4

Post

Temporary brace

SPLICING BEAMS

If you must join two beams end to end, be sure the joint falls over a post, for adequate support. You can make the splice with metal straps or gusset plates that can be purchased, or with cleats made of 2-by stock. Another option is to make the splice with special post caps such as the one shown below, at right.

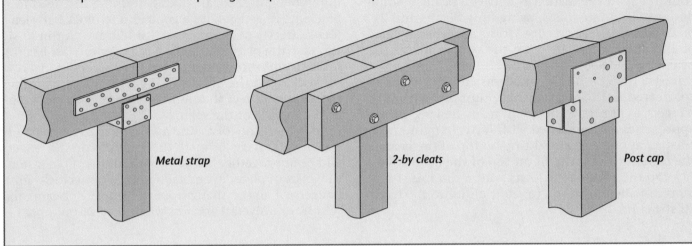

Metal strap   2-by cleats   Post cap

Bracing posts

TOOLKIT

- Combination square
- Circular saw or crosscut saw
- Claw hammer
- Electric drill
- Wrenches

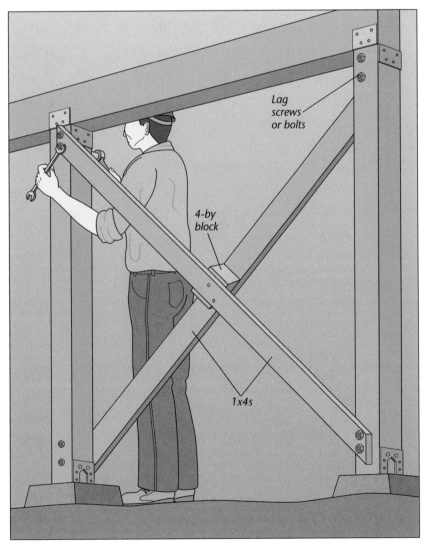

Lag screws or bolts

4-by block

1x4s

Attaching the brace

If your deck's posts will require bracing, it should be installed before you add any more weight to the structure. Mark the individual cross braces in position against the posts, then cut them on the ground.

Temporarily nail the braces in place and then drill pilot holes for bolts or lag screws and fasten the ends of the bracing. To provide support and to fill the spaces between the braces, insert a 4-by block where they cross, as shown at left, and nail it in place.

If you're using pressure-treated wood, don't forget to treat the cut ends and drilled holes with wood preservative.

JOISTS

Deck joists spread decking loads across beams, making it possible to use decking materials that otherwise couldn't span the distances between beams. (Some designs eliminate joists, using only beams and 2x3 or 2x4 decking laid on edge.) Joists are generally made of 2-by lumber and are often the same width as the beam and ledger.

Joists either sit on top of beams and ledgers or are connected to the faces of these supports with joist hangers, as illustrated below. In many designs, the two approaches are combined with joists hanging from a ledger at one end and sitting on top of the beam at the other. If the joists sit on top of the beams, you can cap the ends of the joists with a rim joist for a more finished look and to add rigidity to the overall structure.

Using blocking (*page 60*) to reinforce joists with long spans or wide spacings will keep the joists from twisting or buckling. Local codes determine the need for blocking. In general, it's a good idea to block between joists directly over any beams or ledgers. (A rim joist can take the place of the blocking over the last beam.) Joists spanning more than 8 feet need an additional row of blocking in the middle of the span; joists spanning more than 12 feet should have two rows of blocking in the middle of the span.

To lay out the joists, use a storyboard as explained on the next page, or mark the locations on the ledger and beams together before you install them. To fasten the joists in place, use metal framing connectors—joist hangers when they hang from the ledger or beam, and seismic or universal anchors when they sit on top.

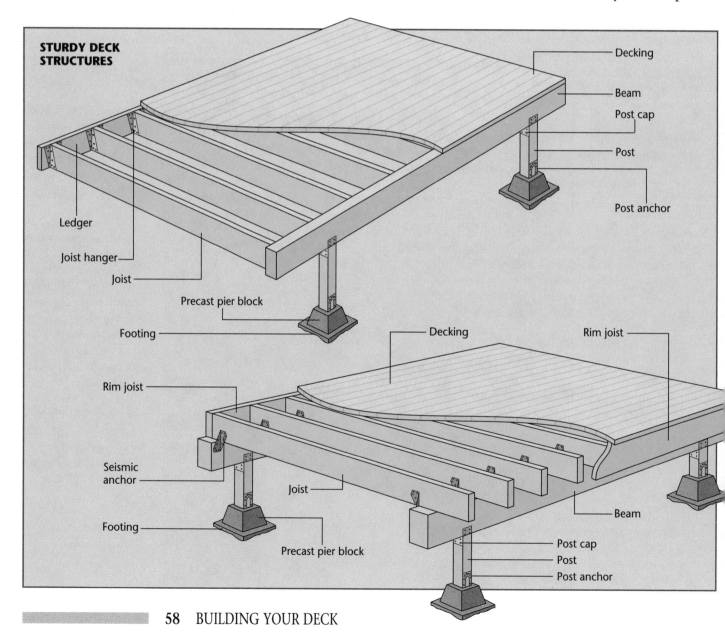

STURDY DECK STRUCTURES

Decking
Beam
Post cap
Post
Post anchor
Ledger
Joist hanger
Joist
Precast pier block
Footing

Rim joist
Decking
Rim joist
Seismic anchor
Joist
Footing
Precast pier block
Beam
Post cap
Post
Post anchor

Installing joists

TOOLKIT
- Tape measure
- Combination square
- Claw hammer
- Circular saw

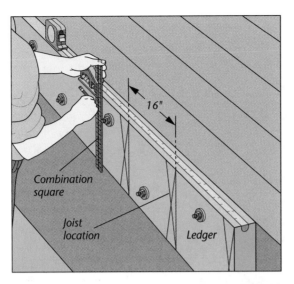

Combination square

Joist location

Ledger

16"

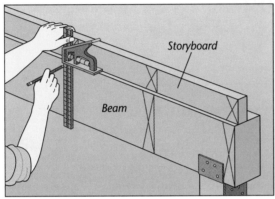

Storyboard

Beam

1 Marking joist locations
Starting at one outside corner of the ledger (or of one beam for a freestanding deck), mark the location of the first joist with an X. For standard 16" centers *(left, above)* hook your tape measure over the end of the beam or ledger and measure 16" to the edge of the next joist; draw a line with a combination square and then an X to indicate which side of the line the joist will fall on. The last interval may be less than 16".

If your decking pattern requires double joists, continue to space the joists every 16" but add an extra joist next to one of the regular ones.

Once the layout is complete, transfer the same spacing to the opposite beam, using a storyboard— a marked length of scrap lumber *(left, below)*.

If you're splicing joists by overlapping them, as described on the next page, the layout on the opposite beam must be offset $1^{1/2}$" to allow for the overlap. Mark the edge of the first joist in from the end at $14^{1/2}$"; then mark every 16".

2 Installing joist hangers
If you're mounting the joists in metal joist hangers, it saves time to get all the hangers in place before mounting any of the joists: Position each hanger so that one side of the opening falls on your layout line and so the joist's top edge will sit flush with the top edge of the ledger or beam (insert a scrap piece of lumber the same size as the joist to align the hanger). Nail this first side to the ledger or beam. Then, squeeze the hanger so it is snug around the scrap of wood, and nail the other side to the ledger or beam. Remove the block and repeat with each hanger.

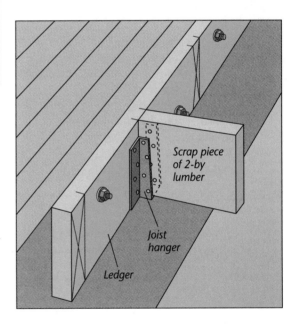

Scrap piece of 2-by lumber

Joist hanger

Ledger

 ASK A PRO

HOW DO I FASTEN THE END JOIST?
If the end joist will come flush to the end of the ledger or beam, you won't have room to put a joist hanger. You can either cut a joist hanger in half, or use a universal framing anchor as shown at right.

For a more finished look, you can have the end joists overlap the ends of the ledger and beam. Cut the end joists longer than the other joists and face-nail them to the ends of the ledger and beam.

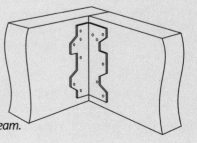

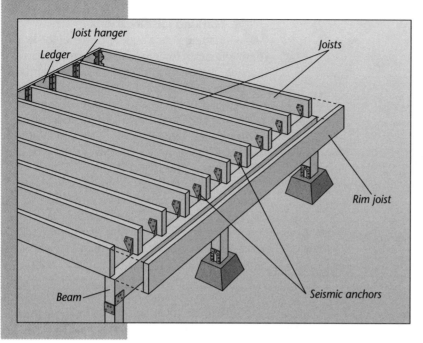

Joist hanger

Ledger

Joists

Rim joist

Beam

Seismic anchors

3 Fastening joists

Measure the distance each joist must span between the beam and the ledger. If the joists will sit in joist hangers, they can be 1/8" to 1/4" short of the proper measurement and still fit. If you find greater discrepancies in distance, you'll have to measure and cut each joist individually; otherwise, you can cut them all to the same length.

If the joists will sit in joist hangers at both ends, simply nail through the hangers into the joists. For joists over 8' long, work with a helper, each lifting one end. If the joists will sit on top of the ledger or beam, line them up with your marks, and fasten each joist with a seismic or universal anchor. Joists should also be fastened to any intermediate beams.

If you're installing a rim joist, face-nail it through the ends of the joists using three or four 3½" nails at each joist. Any joints in the rim joist must fall at a joist end.

SPLICING JOISTS

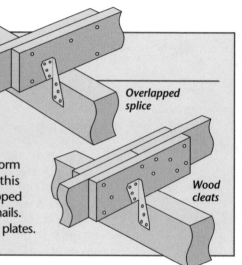

Overlapped splice

Wood cleats

On a large deck, joists must be spliced together. A splice must be supported by a beam; be sure each joist end bears at least a full inch on the beam. If several spliced joists are needed, plan to stagger the splices over different beams to avoid weakening the substructure.

The overlap method of splicing (right, above) is the easiest, but it breaks up uniform spacing—throwing off the alignment of decking end joints later on. If you use this method and more than one splice is needed on a full joist length, alternate overlapped sides. For standard 2-by lumber, nail both faces of each splice with six 3" common nails. To maintain uniform spacing, use wood cleats (right, below) or metal straps or gusset plates.

Blocking joists

TOOLKIT
- Tape measure
- Chalk line
- Combination square
- Circular saw
- Claw hammer

Fastening the blocking

Requirements for blocking are discussed on page 58. Snap a chalk line across the joists at the relevant points, then work your way across the joists, measuring and listing the lengths of blocking you'll need to cut from the joist material. Cut and code all the blocks to correspond to their locations.

It's easiest to alternate the blocks, staggering them from one side of the chalk line to the other (right, above). By using this technique, you'll be able to face-nail the blocks—use 3½" nails.

When you install blocks over beams (right, below) you can face-nail one end of each block, but the other end will have to be toenailed—use 2½" nails.

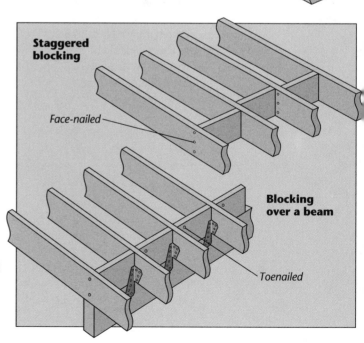

Staggered blocking

Face-nailed

Blocking over a beam

Toenailed

Changes in level add visual interest to your deck and can also define different use areas. In some cases, the second level is merely a landing providing a smooth transition to the house or yard. Shown here are three of the simplest ways of constructing level changes.

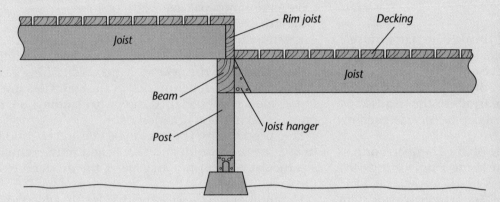

If you want the distance between levels to be only one step—thus avoiding a flight of stairs—you can accomplish this most easily by constructing the upper level with joists resting on top of beams, then using joist hangers for the lower level. This way, the lower joists are at the same level as the tops of the beams and only the width of a joist below the upper level.

For a change in levels of more than one step, you can attach a ledger along the posts of the higher level and use it to support the lower deck's joists. Of course, you'll also have to add steps to link the two levels.

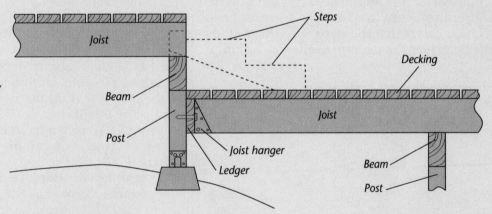

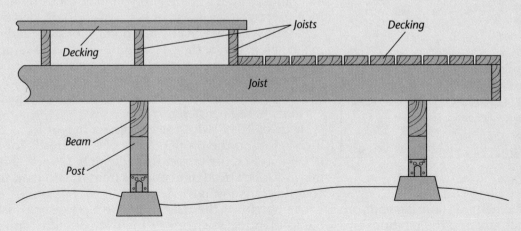

If the upper deck will be very small, create multiple levels by building the framing of the deck as though it were for one level, then adding a second layer of joists (at right angles) on top of the first. This setup offers the advantage of reversing the decking on the two levels, creating a safer visual separation.

STAIRS

Any deck higher than about 10 inches is difficult to step up onto and will require a flight of stairs. Stairs not only provide access to your deck, they can also guide foot traffic, offer extra seating, and, if they run the full length of the deck, can hide the substructure from view.

CONSTRUCTION BASICS

A basic stairway consists of treads (the flat surface on which you step) and risers (the vertical surface). Outdoor stairs most often have open risers. Treads are fastened to a support structure of angle stringers; these can be notched to receive the treads or the treads can rest on wooden cleats or metal connectors fastened to the inside of the stringers.

Stringers are generally made of 2x12 lumber. For narrow stairways, you'll need one stringer supporting each end of the treads. For stairways over 4 feet wide, add a third stringer down the center. For extremely wide steps, plan a stringer every 4 feet. Precut notched stringers can be purchased at a home center.

The choice of lumber for the treads depends on the depth of tread you want to achieve, as discussed below. Visually, you can match the steps with the deck by using the same material for both treads and decking.

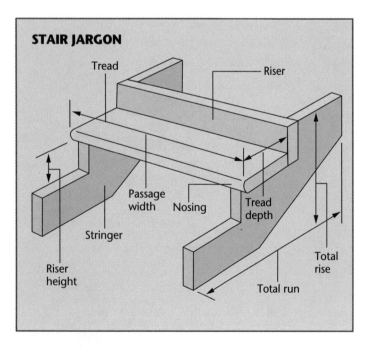

STAIR JARGON

Tread

Riser

Passage width

Nosing

Tread depth

Stringer

Riser height

Total rise

Total run

STAIR DIMENSIONS

The comfort and safety of a flight of stairs depends on the passage width, the total run, and the relationship between the risers and treads. For illustrations of these terms, see above.

Passage width: Decide how much traffic you expect, then base your stairs' passage width on the following minimums for general access: Provide at least 4 feet for one person, or 5 feet for two abreast; add 2 feet per person for greater numbers of side-by-side users. Service stairs or other deliberately restricted access stairs may have a minimum passage width of 2 feet.

Length of run: Stairs for elevation changes up to 8 feet can generally be handled in a single straight, uninterrupted run stretching directly from one level to another. For a higher total rise, a landing makes climbing easier, and a change in direction makes the stairs less imposing. L-shaped or U-shaped runs with landings are recommended in these situations.

Step proportions: For steps to be safe and comfortable to use, the tread width and riser height must maintain a particular relationship: In general, the shorter the riser, the wider the tread.

For outdoor steps, twice the riser height added to the tread width should equal 24 to 26 inches. The ideal riser height is considered to be 6 to 7 inches. If you're building very wide stairs, this may feel too steep; instead, you may want as little as a 4½-inch rise. Keep in mind that shallower stairs will have a longer total run, making them impractical for climbing up to a high deck. Typical tread-to-riser ratios are shown opposite.

Where possible, choose lumber for the treads that will create the right depth of tread without having to rip the boards to size. For example, two 2x6s with a ⅛-inch gap give a tread of 11⅛ inches. For a shallower stairway, you can use three 2x6s to give a tread of about 17 inches.

Measuring for stairs: To determine the number of steps you need, measure the vertical distance (total rise) from the deck to the ground; then divide by the riser height you intend to use. For example, if the deck is 45½ inches above grade and you plan on using 6½-inch risers, you need 7 steps exactly—45½ divided by 6½. If this formula gives you a number of steps ending in a fraction, divide the whole number into the vertical distance to find the exact riser measurements. That is, if the deck is 54 inches above grade, 54 divided by 6½ inches per riser equals 8+ steps; 54 divided by 8 equals 6¾ inches rise per step.

Next, subtract twice the exact riser height from 26 inches to find the proper depth of each tread. For a 6½-inch riser, the proper tread depth is 13 inches—26 minus 13. The tread dimension is from riser to riser, not counting any nosing.

The height of the risers must be as close as possible to identical—within ¼ inch—to avoid tripping. If you must have an odd-sized riser, it should be at the bottom.

TREAD-TO-RISER RATIOS

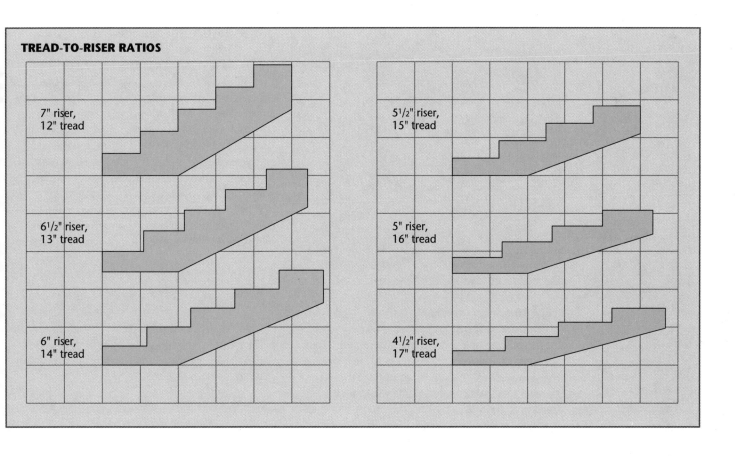

7" riser, 12" tread

6¹/₂" riser, 13" tread

6" riser, 14" tread

5¹/₂" riser, 15" tread

5" riser, 16" tread

4¹/₂" riser, 17" tread

RAMPS

The most obvious use for ramps is, of course, for wheelchair access, but they're also useful for maneuvering baby carriages and wheelbarrows.

In designing a ramp, ease of ascent is critical. A ramp's slope is measured in inches of vertical rise per foot of linear distance, a lower rise allowing an easier ascent. For wheelchair access, construct a ramp with a slope no greater than 1 in 12; for a utility ramp, 1 in 8 will do.

As in stair design, the length of the run is what can make climbing a ramp either pleasant or threatening. Make sure that no straight run creates an elevation change greater than 36 inches. For a higher rise, break the run with a level landing where the user can pause. Try to allow for some change in direction at each landing, although you needn't have dramatic switchbacks.

A ramp is essentially a narrow deck on an incline. Use stringers without notches, and run decking across them. Anchor the bottom of the ramp to a concrete pad as shown at right. Check local codes to see if a handrail is required.

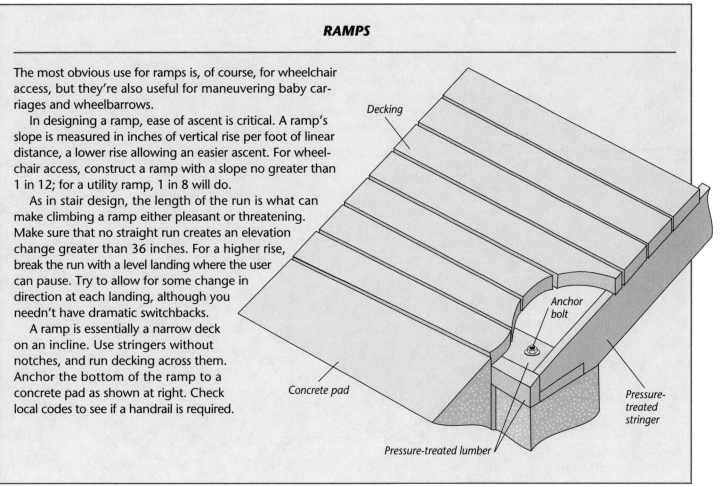

Decking

Anchor bolt

Concrete pad

Pressure-treated stringer

Pressure-treated lumber

TOOLKIT
- Shovel
- Mortar hoe (optional)
- Electric drill
- Wrench
- Carpenter's square and stair gauges
- Circular saw
- Crosscut saw
- Tape measure
- Combination square
- Claw hammer

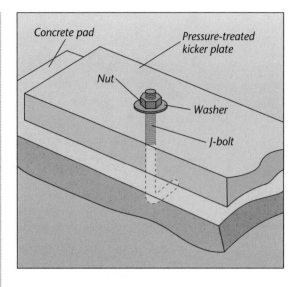

Concrete pad
Pressure-treated kicker plate
Nut
Washer
J-bolt

1 Casting the foundation

To support the bottom of the stringers, cast a concrete pad about 4" deep. First dig a trench, then fill it with concrete, taking care to place the concrete on undisturbed soil. (Turn to page 48 for information on working with concrete.) Cover the concrete with burlap, straw, or newspaper, and keep the covering moist for about a week.

If you're using a kicker plate, as shown at left, set J-bolts in the concrete while it's still wet, leaving about 2 1/2" exposed. When the concrete has cured, drill holes for the bolts in a pressure-treated 2-by board. Place this kicker plate over the exposed bolts, add washers, and tighten the nuts on the outside.

2 Notching stringers

Using stair gauges, mark the riser dimension on the tongue of a carpenter's square; then mark the tread dimension on the square's body. Line up the gauges with the top edge of the stringer, as shown below, and trace the outline of the riser and tread onto the stringer. Move the square along to mark the rest of the notches. Because the tread's thickness will add to the height of the first step, you'll need to subtract this amount from the bottom of the stringer as illustrated.

Cut out the notches with a circular saw, finishing each cut with a crosscut saw. (NOTE: If you're using a kicker plate, you'll have to notch the bottom of the stringer to fit around it.) Once your pattern is cut, hold it in position against the deck to check the alignment; if it's satisfactory, use the stringer you've just cut as a template for marking the others (*inset*).

Cleated stringers are laid out in the same way, but instead of notching the stringer, you attach wood cleats, or metal stair angles as shown on page 26.

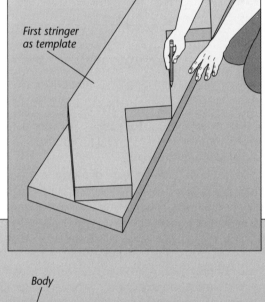

First stringer as template

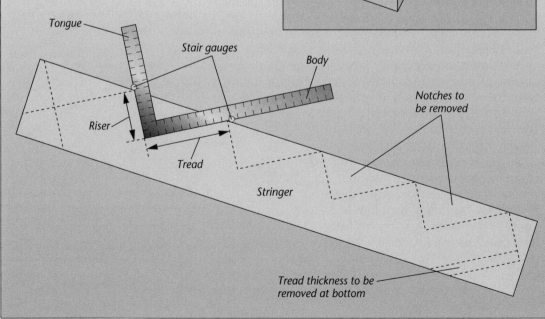

Tongue
Stair gauges
Body
Riser
Tread
Stringer
Notches to be removed
Tread thickness to be removed at bottom

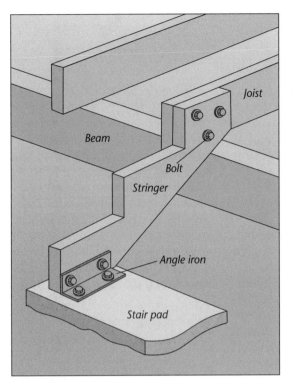

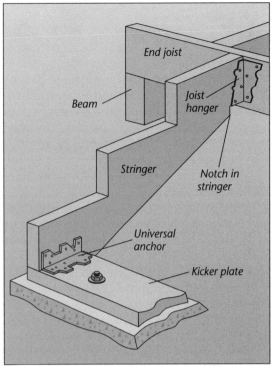

3 Fastening the stringers

If the ends of the joists are exposed on the side of the deck where you want to install the stairs, bolt the tops of the stringers to them as shown (*above, left*). Otherwise, attach the stringers to the end joist or rim joist using joist hangers—the stringers will have to be notched to accommodate the connector (*above, right*). You'll then have to attach the bottom of the stringers to the concrete pad. If you haven't installed a kicker plate, fasten the stringers to the pad with angle irons. Using a masonry bit, drill holes for expanding anchor bolts or expansion shields (*page 24*) and tap the bolts or shields into the concrete. Fasten the angle irons to the pad and then to the stringer. If you have a kicker plate, attach the stringers to it with angle irons or universal anchors.

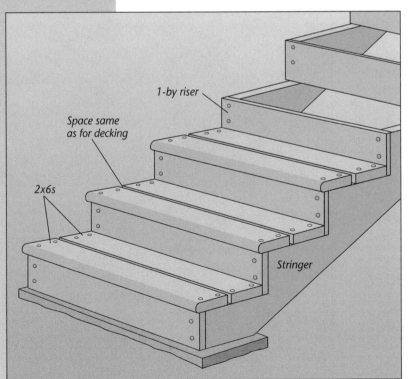

4 Adding treads and risers

When measuring and cutting treads and risers, remember that the bottom edge of a riser tucks behind the back of the tread, and the forward edge of the tread overlaps the riser below it. Giving each tread a 1" nosing (a projection beyond the front of the riser) lends a more finished appearance to the stairway.

Nail risers to the stringers first, using 3$1/4$" nails, then nail the treads to the stringers; use two nails at each end of the boards. Use a nail to space the tread boards $1/8$" to $3/16$" apart (use the same spacing as you will use for the decking). Finally, working under the stairway, fasten the bottom edges of the risers to the backs of the treads. For cleated stringers, simply fasten the treads and risers to the cleats.

DECKING

The surface is the most noticeable part of your deck and the way it's designed will establish the deck's character. The pattern of the decking can be varied by the size of lumber you choose and the way it's laid as discussed below. For information on installing decking, turn to page 68.

DECKING DESIGN

In many cases, a simple arrangement is the best choice: decking lumber set parallel, perpendicular, or diagonal to the deck's long axis. These simple patterns create an illusion of size because the eye is drawn beyond the deck rather than encouraged to focus on design detail. More involved patterns such as herringbone or mitered can be effective if you coordinate them with other surface textures or if they relate to architectural features of your house. However, there are some instances where a complex pattern wouldn't work; for example, between a shingled house and a flagstone walkway, anything but a simple pattern of parallel boards would introduce an unsettling distraction. To evaluate possible decking patterns, sketch them on tracing paper laid on top of your scale drawing of the deck's shape.

Generally speaking, the more complex the decking pattern, the more complicated the substructure must be to support it. A diagonal pattern requires setting joists closer together; more elaborate designs call for doubling joists at regular intervals to permit nailing of abutting lumber. (Examples of the framework required for various decking patterns are illustrated opposite.) Spacing between supports is also affected by the lumber's thickness, grade, and species. For information on the correct spacing of supports, refer to the span charts on page 41.

Most decks are surfaced with standard sizes of dimension lumber: surfaced 2x6s, 2x4s, or 2x3s. You'll find that 2x2s tend to twist and warp easily unless they are redwood or cedar; 2x8s (and anything larger) tend to cup and drain poorly. The most common choice is 2x6s—they can be laid faster than narrower boards, offer more room for fastening, and warp less.

The simplest, soundest, and most economical decking patterns are those in which 2x6s or 2x4s are laid parallel, running the deck's full length or width; however, you can also mix lumber of two or more different widths, such as 2x4s and 2x6s as shown at right.

Patterns created by laying 2x3s or 2x4s on their edges, usually directly on beams (without joists), are alternatives to the standard flat decking. On-edge decking is heavy and expensive, but it can span longer distances between supports—an advantage if you want to pare down the substructure. Be aware, though, that the added expense of this sort of decking pattern generally isn't offset by the substructure savings. Fastening the ends of on-edge decking requires more nailing surface than flat decking; if the joints don't fall over a large beam, locate them over a double joist, or attach cleats to the sides of the joists to increase the nailing surface. On-edge decking should be separated with spacers as shown below, both over the supports and in the middle of the spans. Spacers should be made of $1/8$"x3"x$3^{1}/2$" exterior-rated, pressure-treated plywood. Coat the spacers in waterproof construction adhesive and face-nail the boards together through the spacers.

Whether you're planning to lay the deck boards flat or on edge, turn to page 21 for information on estimating how much decking lumber you'll need for your design.

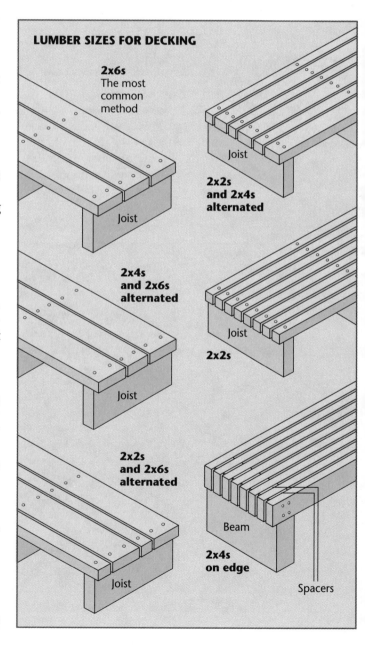

LUMBER SIZES FOR DECKING

2x6s
The most common method

2x2s and 2x4s alternated

Joist

2x4s and 2x6s alternated

Joist

2x2s

2x2s and 2x6s alternated

Joist

2x4s on edge

Beam

Spacers

SIMPLE DECKING PATTERNS

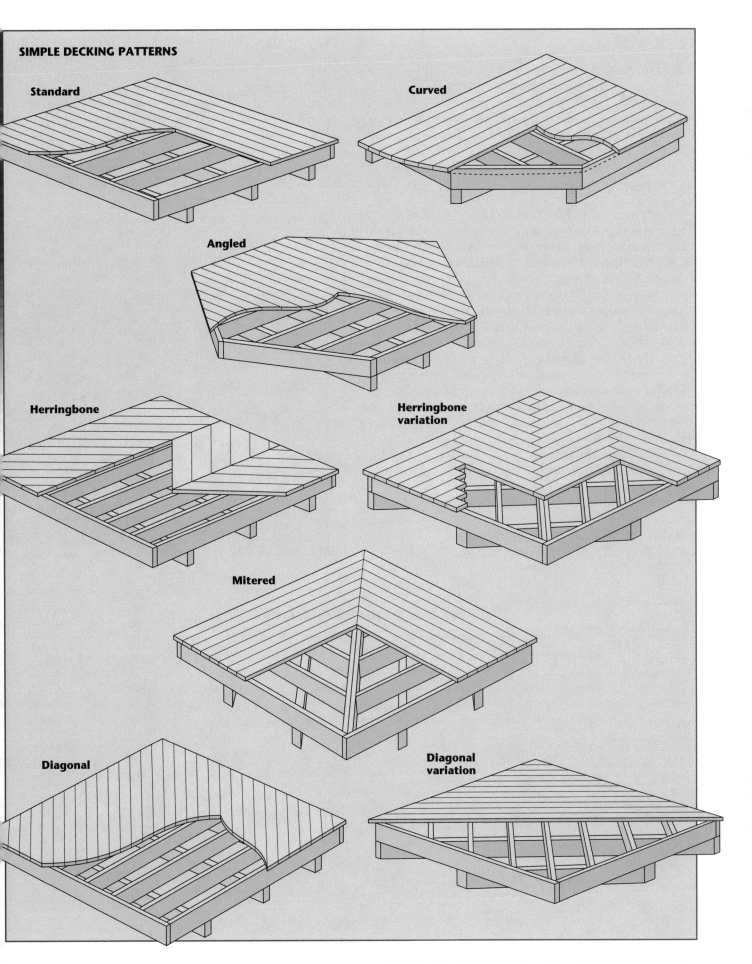

Standard

Curved

Angled

Herringbone

Herringbone variation

Mitered

Diagonal

Diagonal variation

INSTALLATION

Decking can be fastened to joists with nails, screws, or special clips. Nailing is the cheapest and quickest method, but screws hold better. For information on choosing the right fastener, turn to page 22. For extra holding power, you can apply construction adhesive in addition to the nails or screws—it is applied to the joists with a caulking gun before the deck boards are laid down. Keep in mind that the boards will be nearly impossible to remove once the adhesive sets—a potential problem if you must make repairs later.

If you're using nails to fasten down decking, hand-nailing is favored for best results. While an air-powered nail gun (pneumatic nailer) will make quicker work of the job than using a hammer, the nails it shoots tend to sink into the wood a little too far, especially in the softer woods such as redwood and cedar. To drive screws, use a screw gun or an electric drill with the appropriate bit.

Fasten deck boards at every support point (joist or beam). Fastening requirements depend on whether you are using pressure-treated lumber, or redwood or cedar, since redwood and cedar are less prone to warping. Consult the illustration at right for the correct pattern for your lumber. Some manufacturers of pressure-treated wood recommend using three nails at each joint for extra strength.

Redwood and cedar boards should be spaced about $1/8$ to $3/16$ inch apart to allow for drainage, ventilation, and the natural expansion and contraction of the wood. Most pressure-treated wood, however, has not been dried after treatment and will tend to shrink as it dries. With this wood, butt the edges. With pressure-treated wood that has been dried after treat-

ment, leave $1/8$- to $3/16$-inch gaps. If possible, choose spacing that will allow you to fit an even number of boards. In all cases, butt the ends of the boards.

If you intend to apply a finish to your deck boards, it's a good idea to do this before you install them. This allows you to get at all sides of the boards. For information on finishing, turn to page 87. If you're using pressure-treated lumber, be sure to brush the cut ends with wood preservative. If you plan to apply a finish to your substructure, do so before the decking is laid.

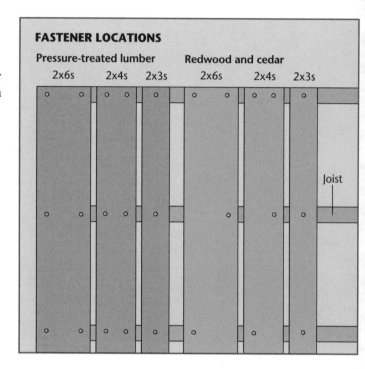

FASTENER LOCATIONS

Pressure-treated lumber: 2x6s, 2x4s, 2x3s
Redwood and cedar: 2x6s, 2x4s, 2x3s

Joist

PLANNING JOINTS IN DECKING

Lumber is available in lengths from 8 to 16 feet in 2-foot increments (20-foot lumber can be special-ordered). A deck less than 16 feet can be built with no joints in the decking. A longer deck will have end joints. Three ways to lay out end joints are shown. Random or alternating joints are the strongest, while grouped joints create a pattern that calls attention to itself. For maximum strength, deck boards should span at least three joists without a joint.

Note: You can minimize waste by designing your deck with deck boards in standard lumber lengths.

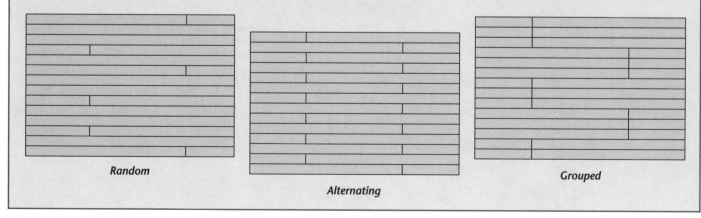

Random

Alternating

Grouped

TOOLKIT
- Tape measure
- Combination square
- Circular saw
- Caulking gun for adhesive (optional)
- Claw hammer, screw gun, or electric drill with screwdriver bit
- Nailset
- Chalk line

Spacing nail

Joist

Joist

1 Fastening the boards

For an attached deck, begin laying decking at the house wall, leaving about a $1/8$" gap between the wall and the first board. Let the decking boards run long—you'll be cutting them off later. If the appearance of the lumber permits, lay the boards bark side up to minimize checking and cupping. (The bark side is the convex side of the board.)

Fasten the boards to each joist, following the pattern given on the previous page. (If you're using adhesive in addition to the nails or screws, apply it to each joist with a caulking gun before setting the boards in place.) To avoid hammer dents, stop hammering as soon as the nail is flush with the decking.

If the boards split as they're being nailed, blunt the tip of each nail with a tap of the hammer and then angle the nails slightly toward the center of the boards. If this doesn't work, drill pilot holes three-quarters of the diameter of the nail shanks.

For decking that requires spacing (pressure-treated lumber that has been dried after treatment, red-wood, and cedar), you can use $3\,1/2$" nails to space decking quickly and uniformly. Use two nails, one at each end of the board already secured; set the nails snugly against the board and push their tips into the joist. Push the next board against the nails, secure it, and pull out the two spacing nails. To keep the nail from slipping down, you can nail it through a small block of wood *(inset)*. For different spacing, use a larger or smaller nail, or cut a spacer from wood; commercial plastic spacers designed for decking are also available.

As you fasten the decking, occasionally check the remaining distance to be covered, measuring from both ends of the decking. If possible, re-adjust the spacing slightly to be able to fit the last board; if a large adjustment will be required, rip the last board to fit.

When the deck is completely nailed, set the head of each nail slightly below the surface with a large nailset.

 ASK A PRO

CAN I USE A BOWED BOARD?

When you're laying decking, you'll find that some boards are too bowed to align properly. To correct the problem, first nail each end of the board to the joists. Then start the nails at their proper locations in the bowed area, over the joists. If the board bows away from the neighboring board, drive a chisel into the joist at the bow's apex (angle the chisel slightly), then pry the board into place and nail as shown. If the board bows toward an adjoining length of decking, force a chisel between the two and pry the bowed board outward, then nail.

Special tools are available to lever bowed boards into place. Some lock in place, leaving both hands free to fasten the board down.

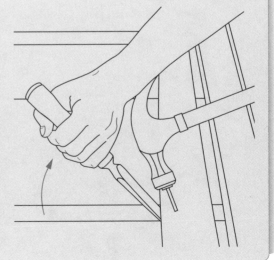

2 Trimming the boards

Once all the boards are nailed down, snap a chalk line carefully along the deck edges and saw along it (you can leave the deck boards cantilevered a couple of inches if you wish). Skilled hands can saw freehand along a chalk line; less experienced builders will want to guide the saw with a length of wood tacked to the deck.

Chalk line

ACCOMMODATING NATURE

Think twice before you remove an intrusive boulder or cut down a tree that happens to be in your planned deck-building area. Instead, consider how your deck might be enhanced by including such natural features as elements in your plan.

There are two approaches to building around a tree or rock. In both cases, you first build a frame around the object, installing double headers. Then, either lay decking to the edge of the frame, or make a custom-fitted cutout by scribing the decking with a compass.

Whenever you surround a tree with decking, remember to allow space for the trunk to enlarge as the tree grows. And never attach lumber to the trunk: This is bad for the tree, and the tree's movement in wind will damage the deck. If you allow a generous opening, consider incorporating a bench into the plan, providing shaded seating.

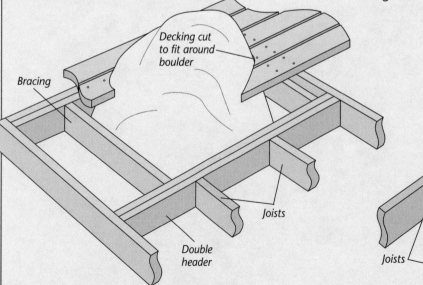

Bracing

Decking cut to fit around boulder

Joists

Double header

Square opening to allow for tree growth

Bracing

Joists

RAILINGS

If your deck is over 30 inches high (above the ground or above a lower level of the deck), most building codes call for a railing. However, rails make any raised deck more secure, especially for small children.

Railings are generally a minimum of 36 inches high; however, a higher railing—up to 42 inches—feels safer. For railings on a deck higher than 30 inches, code generally requires that there be no gaps in the structure big enough to accept a sphere bigger than 4 inches (although some codes allow 6 inches); this will prevent children from injuring themselves. Railings must be built strong enough to resist a hefty horizontal force (up to 20 pounds per square foot). Be sure to consult your building department for any local requirements.

Railings all have the same basic structure: vertical posts joined by a cross member at the top, with the space between the posts filled in with horizontal rails, vertical balusters, or both. (If you have active small children, try to design a railing that will be difficult to climb.) The strongest railings are those connected to posts that extend up from the deck's substructure. This will require designing your deck with sandwiched beams

or posts *(page 53)*. Typical attachment methods for independent railing posts are shown below. Railings that come up through the decking are best installed before the decking, while railings fastened to the outside of the deck structure can be installed before or after the decking.

Post spacing is related to the size of the top cross member: A 2x4 laid flat can span 4 feet; a 2x6 can span up to 6 feet. A top cross member placed on edge can span longer distances. The combination of a 2x4 rail on edge and a cap can span up to 8 feet—and the cap protects the end grain on the tops of the posts from water. If no cap is used, cut the tops at an angle to shed water.

Horizontal rails may be fastened to the faces of the posts, attached between them with metal angles or wood cleats, or placed in dadoes in the posts. Balusters are generally fastened to the outside face of the top rail and the bottom rail, rim joist, or fascia.

Well-designed railings provide safety and enhance a deck's appearance. You can coordinate railings with the house by using similar materials and detailing. Some simple designs are shown on the next page.

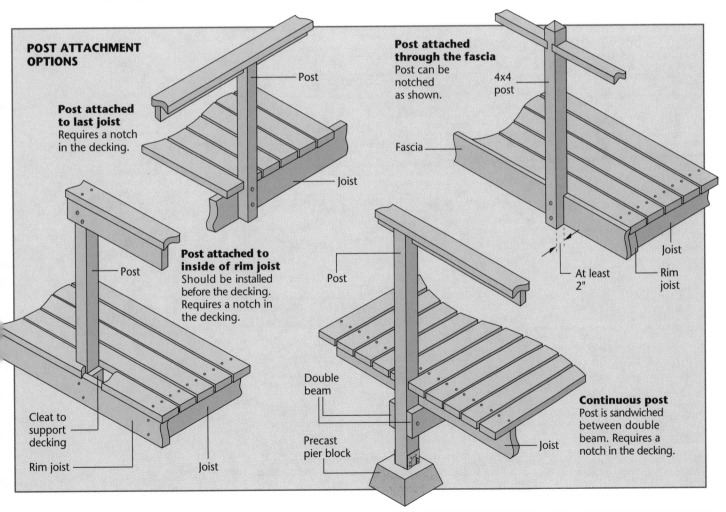

POST ATTACHMENT OPTIONS

Post attached to last joist
Requires a notch in the decking.

Post

Joist

Post

Post attached to inside of rim joist
Should be installed before the decking. Requires a notch in the decking.

Cleat to support decking

Rim joist

Joist

Post attached through the fascia
Post can be notched as shown.

4x4 post

Fascia

Joist

At least 2"

Rim joist

Post

Double beam

Precast pier block

Joist

Continuous post
Post is sandwiched between double beam. Requires a notch in the decking.

BASIC RAILING DESIGNS

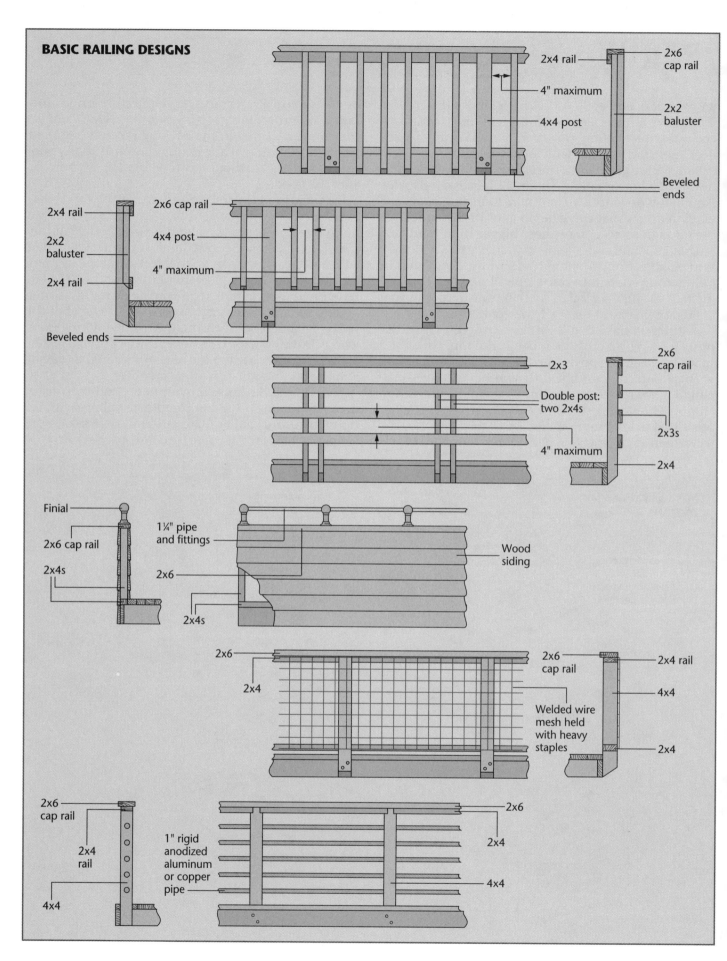

2x4 rail

2x6 cap rail

4" maximum

4x4 post

2x2 baluster

Beveled ends

2x4 rail

2x6 cap rail

2x2 baluster

4x4 post

4" maximum

2x4 rail

Beveled ends

2x3

Double post: two 2x4s

4" maximum

2x6 cap rail

2x3s

2x4

Finial

2x6 cap rail

2x4s

1¼" pipe and fittings

2x6

2x4s

Wood siding

2x6

2x4

2x6 cap rail

2x4 rail

4x4

Welded wire mesh held with heavy staples

2x4

2x6 cap rail

2x4 rail

4x4

2x6 cap rail

2x4 rail

4x4

1" rigid anodized aluminum or copper pipe

2x6

2x4

4x4

Any stairway with more than three risers requires a handrail for people to hold onto. The handrail should be easy to grip; generally a 2-by on edge is best. This means leaving the posts uncapped—cut the ends on angle to shed water and treat the exposed end grain.

In addition, stairs with a total rise of 30 inches or more require a complete railing that meets the same design requirements as the deck perimeter railings described on page 71. Most codes allow only 4 inches between rails (6 inches is acceptable for the triangle under the lowest rail). Measured from the top of the railing to the top front edges of the treads as shown at right, the railing height must be at least 30 inches, at most 34 inches (check your building code). Posts should be bolted or lag screwed to the stringers, and never to the stair treads.

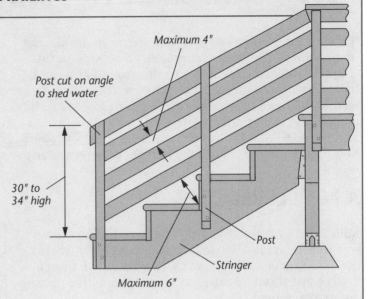

Maximum 4"

Post cut on angle to shed water

30" to 34" high

Post

Stringer

Maximum 6"

Assembling the railings

TOOLKIT
- Tape measure
- Combination square
- Circular saw
- Crosscut saw (optional)
- Butt chisel
- Claw hammer
- Electric drill
- Wrenches
- Screwdriver (optional)
- Power miter saw or table saw (optional)
- Hand-drilling hammer

1 ▶ Attaching the posts
Cut the posts to length using a circular saw—for 4x4 posts you may have to finish the cuts with a crosscut saw. If the rails will fit into dadoes in the posts, cut the dadoes now. If you have to notch the decking, mark the notch and then make the cuts with a butt chisel (*right*).

Drill holes for bolts and bolt the posts to the deck substructure (*inset*); you can use any of the attachment methods shown on page 71.

NOTE: If the post will penetrate through the decking and the end of a deck board will be left unsupported, install a cleat on the post for the board to rest on.

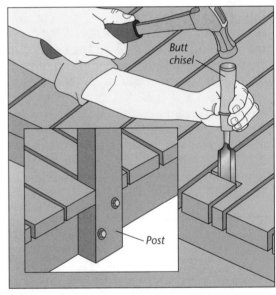

Butt chisel

Post

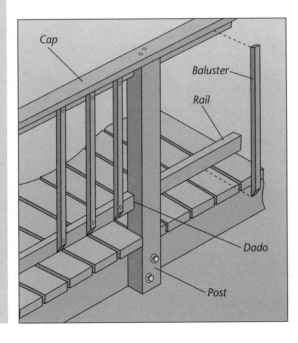

Cap

Baluster

Rail

Dado

Post

2 Completing the railing
First, add the cap, fastening it to each post with two 3" screws, or 3¼" or 3½" nails. Use the longest lumber available so that the cap will be supported by as many posts as possible. At corners, make a miter joint.

If the rails are set into dadoes in the posts as shown at left, tap them into place and secure them with two 3¼" or 3½" nails. As with the cap, use the longest lumber available.

Use a power miter saw or table saw to cut the balusters to length; you can also bevel the ends as shown. Fasten the balusters with one 3" nail or screw at each end. To avoid knocking the rails off as you hammer, hold them in place with a hand-drilling hammer.

TWO SIMPLE DECK PLANS

The two deck plans shown here are quite simple, but include all the basic components discussed in this chapter. The first deck is low to the ground and can be built either freestanding or attached to the house. The second, higher deck incorporates a railing and stairs. If you choose to build from either of these plans, you'll likely need to adapt it to suit your exact situation. Keep in mind that if you change the number or length of any

of the structural members you'll have to ensure that the spans involved are still acceptable—consult the charts on page 41 and 42. The type of lumber you choose to use will also affect the allowable spans.

Before you begin to build, be sure to check your plan with local building authorities and get any required permits; specifications such as depth of footings or spacing between rails vary from one area to the next.

A LOW-LEVEL DECK

Building a low deck like this one is a quick and easy way to add an outdoor floor to your yard. Because this deck is so small—only 8 feet by 12 feet—it will fit in a yard of just about any size, providing you with a pleasant garden retreat.

For the foundation, use precast piers with post anchors. On sloping terrain, as shown here, you'll need posts supporting the deck at the low end; cut the posts to the length required to make the deck level on your slope. At the high end, you can place the beam directly on the piers. If the terrain is level, you can omit all the posts, placing the beams right in the piers' post anchors.

To build a higher deck from this plan, use longer posts between the piers and the beams. To add a step, use 6x6 pressure-treated landscape timbers, a large flat rock, or a concrete slab where you want to access the deck. Check your local building code for the maximum deck height allowed before you have to add a railing; generally, it's 30 inches.

MATERIALS LIST	
Use pressure-treated lumber for the structural members; decay-resistant lumber such as cedar or redwood heartwood, or pressure-treated wood for the decking; and corrosion-resistant hardware.	
Lumber	
Posts	4x4
Beams	4x8
Joists	2x6
Decking	2x6
Fascia	2x10
Masonry	
Pier blocks	Precast concrete
Concrete	12" square footings
Hardware	
Nails	$3^1/_4$" or $3^1/_2$" for decking; nails for framing connectors
Connectors	Post caps; joist hangers; universal anchors

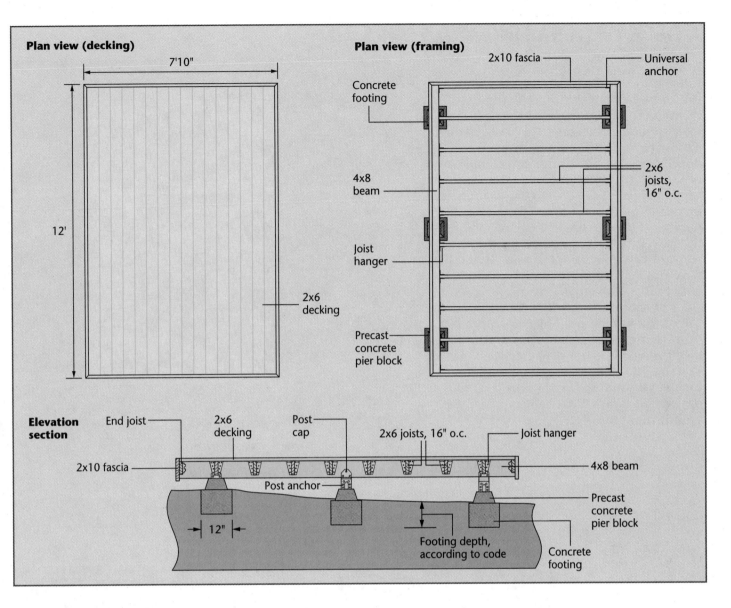

Plan view (decking)

7'10"

12'

2x6 decking

Plan view (framing)

2x10 fascia

Universal anchor

Concrete footing

4x8 beam

2x6 joists, 16" o.c.

Joist hanger

Precast concrete pier block

Elevation section

End joist

2x6 decking

Post cap

2x6 joists, 16" o.c.

Joist hanger

2x10 fascia

4x8 beam

Post anchor

12"

Footing depth, according to code

Precast concrete pier block

Concrete footing

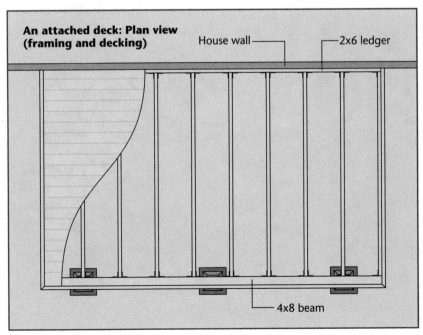

An attached deck: Plan view (framing and decking)

House wall

2x6 ledger

4x8 beam

FOR AN ATTACHED DECK

To attach this deck to your house, replace one of the beams with a ledger attached to the house, as shown in the illustration at left. For information on attaching a ledger to different wall materials, see the section on mounting a ledger *(page 44)*.

A DECK WITH RAILING AND STAIRS

Angling a deck off a house makes it more interesting visually, and in this case, permits for a large deck surface with the least intrusion into yard space. Although it overlooks a small garden here, this design would also work well in the woods, or as an entry. Build it on any side of the house, at a corner, or nestled into an L.

The height of the deck is easily adjusted by changing the size of the posts and the number of steps or size of the risers. Without the posts, this deck can be built just a step above garden level. If you choose to raise the deck to more than 30 inches, a guard rail will likely be required on both sides of the stairs—consult local codes.

Railings are required by code for decks over 30 inches high, but they are a good idea even on a lower deck like this one. You should round the inside corners of the cap rail for comfort. Rout out the back side of the stair handrail to create a finger grip as shown on page 77.

MATERIALS LIST	
Designed for pressure-treated lumber (structural members), surfaced redwood (visible members), and galvanized hardware.	
Lumber	
Posts	4x4
Beams	4x8
Joists	2x6
Blocking	2x6 atop beams and ledgers, and at bench and rail posts
Ledgers	4x8 for deck; 2x4 for benches
Decking	2x6
Fascia	2x8
Stairs	2x12 stringers; 2x6 treads; 2x4 risers
Railings	4x4 posts; 2x6 cap, stair handrail; 2x8 rails; 2x4 stretchers; 1½" dowel; ½" benderboard
Masonry	
Pier blocks	12" precast concrete
Concrete	18"x18" post footings; 18"x6' stair pad, 12" deep
Hardware	
Nails and screws	3½" nails or deck screws; nails for framing connectors; ³⁄₈"x6" lag screws for handrail
Bolts	⅝" bolts for ledgers and sandwiched blocking; ½" bolts at all other vertical connections to posts
Connectors	Post anchors; post caps; angled joist hangers at beam to ledger; sloped joist hangers at top of stringers; 8"x8"x2" angle irons at foot of stringer; seismic anchors at joist to beam

Design: Ann Christoph, ASLA, Landscape Architect

Plan view of framing, foundation and decking

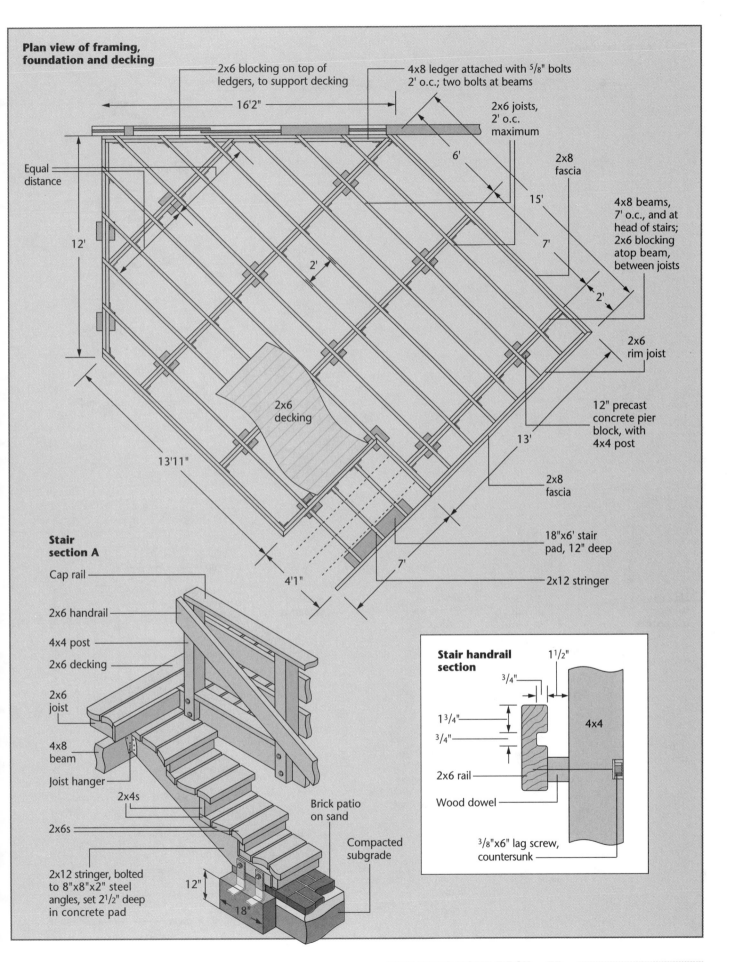

2x6 blocking on top of ledgers, to support decking

4x8 ledger attached with 5/8" bolts 2' o.c.; two bolts at beams

16'2"

2x6 joists, 2' o.c. maximum

6'

2x8 fascia

4x8 beams, 7' o.c., and at head of stairs; 2x6 blocking atop beam, between joists

Equal distance

15'

7'

12'

2'

2'

2x6 rim joist

2x6 decking

12" precast concrete pier block, with 4x4 post

13'11"

13'

2x8 fascia

18"x6' stair pad, 12" deep

4'1"

7'

2x12 stringer

Stair section A

Cap rail

2x6 handrail

4x4 post

2x6 decking

2x6 joist

4x8 beam

Joist hanger

2x4s

2x6s

2x12 stringer, bolted to 8"x8"x2" steel angles, set 2 1/2" deep in concrete pad

Brick patio on sand

Compacted subgrade

12"

18"

Stair handrail section

1 1/2"

3/4"

1 3/4"

3/4"

4x4

2x6 rail

Wood dowel

3/8"x6" lag screw, countersunk

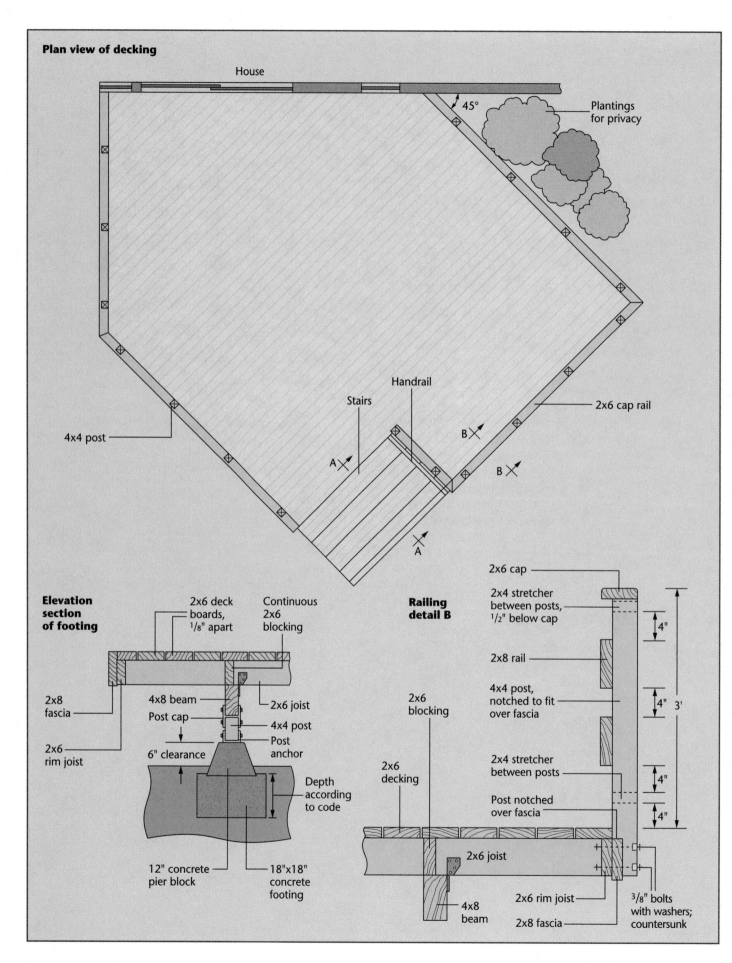

Plan view of decking

House

45°

Plantings for privacy

Stairs

Handrail

A

B

B

B

A

4x4 post

2x6 cap rail

Elevation section of footing

2x6 deck boards, 1/8" apart

Continuous 2x6 blocking

4x8 beam

2x6 joist

2x8 fascia

Post cap

4x4 post

Post anchor

2x6 rim joist

6" clearance

Depth according to code

12" concrete pier block

18"x18" concrete footing

Railing detail B

2x6 cap

2x4 stretcher between posts, 1/2" below cap

2x8 rail

4x4 post, notched to fit over fascia

2x4 stretcher between posts

Post notched over fascia

2x6 blocking

2x6 decking

2x6 joist

4x8 beam

2x6 rim joist

2x8 fascia

3/8" bolts with washers; countersunk

4"

4"

4"

4"

3'

FINISHING TOUCHES

You can create an outdoor environment that's uniquely suited to your lifestyle and taste by integrating amenities, such as lighting, overheads, benches, and planters, into your deck. And even if you don't add any of these touches, the final step in the building process is to apply a finish, to keep your deck looking good and to prolong its life.

In this chapter, we'll show you a variety of options for your deck. Outdoor lighting and plumbing are discussed on the following page. Some screens and overhead designs are provided beginning on page 81: A well-placed screen can reduce the effects of strong winds and provide privacy, while an overhead—even one with a very open cover—can create welcome shade. You'll find some bench styles illustrated on page 84, and storage ideas on page 85: By building your own benches you'll be sure they harmonize with your deck—and you can build a handy storage compartment right into the bench. Planters, either built-in or freestanding, let you bring the garden to your deck, and help integrate the structure with the landscaping; to design your own planter, turn to page 86. Finally, for information on protecting your deck from the damaging effects of exposure, see page 87.

Even before your deck is built, it's important to consider any additions you may want, because they may affect the planning and building stages. For example, one way to build an overhead is to extend the deck's posts above the decking to the required height. You have to decide this before you build your deck, since it affects not only the overall length of the posts, but the method of attaching the beams as well.

Increase your storage space with a hidden compartment under your deck.

PLUMBING AND LIGHTING

Adding plumbing or lighting will enhance your enjoyment of your deck. With the addition of plumbing, your options for outdoor comfort and convenience will be broadened; by installing lights, the length of time that you can spend outdoors will be increased.

Plumbing: For routine deck maintenance, you'll want at least one hose connection nearby. You may also choose to install an outdoor shower or sink, or a fountain, pool, or spa. Whether you can make these additions yourself depends on your plumbing skill and experience: If you're new to plumbing, you'll probably want professional help, but if you're experienced and handy, you'll probably find installing an outdoor faucet a relatively easy job. In any case, check your local building code regulations—water supply systems for decks may require a permit.

If your deck is high enough to provide easy access to the substructure, you can install pipes after construction is complete. This will allow you to live with your deck long enough to get a good idea of where you want the plumbing fixtures located. On a lower deck, it's most convenient to install the pipes during initial construction.

Lighting: You can either install a 12-volt system or extend your home's 120-volt system. A 12-volt (low-voltage) system is more energy efficient, much easier to install, and much less likely to cause harmful shock than a 120-volt system. You can buy a low-voltage deck lighting system as a kit from a home center or hardware store. The kits include a transformer, to change your home's current to 12 volts, post-style lights, and cable. You may also want a timer, which will turn the lights on and off automatically. In most areas, no permit is required to install this type of lighting. You'll need an exterior outlet protected with a ground fault circuit interrupter (GFCI), a safety device that quickly cuts off power if a current leak is detected. Plug the transformer into the GFCI-protected outlet and run the outdoor cable to the fixtures, following the manufacturer's instructions; no grounding connections are required.

Installing a 120-volt system is more complicated and requires hiring an electrician, but it has some advantages over a low-voltage system: Light can be projected much farther, and outlets can be added so you can use power tools and other electrical devices outdoors.

Whatever system you plan to install, check with your local building department to see if you need a permit for the electrical work.

PIPING WATER TO YOUR DECK

Existing pipe
Faucet
Elbows
Pipe straps
Drain valve
Tee
Coupling
Coupling

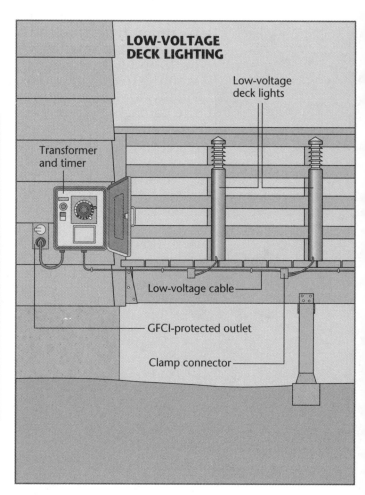

LOW-VOLTAGE DECK LIGHTING

Low-voltage deck lights
Transformer and timer
Low-voltage cable
GFCI-protected outlet
Clamp connector

SCREENS

Adding a screen can dramatically change the environment of your deck: You can use it to block out a view you don't like, as well as to block the view onto your deck, providing a sense of privacy. A well-placed screen can mitigate the effects of a strong wind, turning your deck into a calm haven.

Screens may be made of a variety of materials, either intricate or simple. Screens used both for wind protection and privacy tend to include lattice panels or other openwork designs; the lattice breaks the wind into a number of more gentle breezes and the intricacy of the design blocks the view. If you're not concerned with blocking a view, you can choose a screen made of transparent material such as acrylic or glass panels—be sure to check your local building code regulations for any restrictions on the use of glass outdoors. A solid barrier is not the best protection against strong winds; an angled baffle at the top will provide better protection for a greater distance on the lee side of the barrier. The drawings at right illustrate two possibilities for screens: a typical wood lattice screen and a screen made of transparent panels (plastic or tempered glass) in a wood frame.

Screens must be firmly fastened to the substructure of the deck. If the screen and the deck are built at the same time, they can be designed so that the support posts of the deck are used as the posts for the screen. This requires that the deck posts extend up through the decking to the height required for the screen. To see how this can be done, turn to page 53.

Screen construction is essentially the same as railing construction; turn to page 71 for more information.

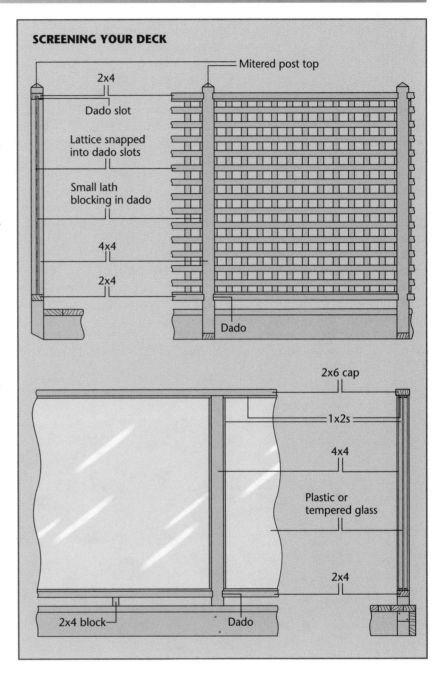

SCREENING YOUR DECK

Mitered post top
2x4
Dado slot
Lattice snapped into dado slots
Small lath blocking in dado
4x4
2x4
Dado

2x6 cap
1x2s
4x4
Plastic or tempered glass
2x4
2x4 block
Dado

ASK A PRO

HOW CAN I HIDE THE SUBSTRUCTURE OF MY DECK?

A lattice screen is an effective visual barrier, whether it's used above the deck to block the view, or below the deck to hide the substructure. If built below the deck, a screen is usually called a skirt. Each section should be anchored to the posts, and a joist or beam. At the bottom, fasten a support board between the posts and attach the skirt sections to it. The skirt will also create a storage area below the deck, and help anchor the deck visually to the ground; this effect is especially welcome on hillside and upper-story decks, which can have a long-legged look if the substructure is exposed.

OVERHEADS

An overhead can shelter your deck from the sun, and provide a sense of privacy and enclosure. When designing one, make sure it won't block any desirable views from the deck or from inside the house. You may not want to cover your entire deck with an overhead; instead you can use it to define a use area, such as a shady area for children to play. Keep in mind that a good overhead design should take its cue from your home's architectural style. Before you begin this building project, be sure to check with the local building department for any restrictions that may apply to your design.

The structure of an overhead is essentially the same as that of a deck. The overhead can be attached to the house with a ledger, as shown below, or it can be free-standing, as shown opposite. In either case, the overhead is supported by a series of posts. It is critical that these posts be solidly attached. The most secure way of achieving this is to design the overhead posts as a continuation of the deck posts. If you're adding an overhead to an existing deck, bolt the overhead posts to the deck's substructure, placing them directly above

or adjacent to the deck posts. The overhead posts support rafters, the equivalent of joists on a deck. If the overhead is attached to the house, the ledger takes the place of a beam, supporting the rafters directly.

Overhead rafters can be left open or can be covered with one of a number of materials. Two very common materials used are narrow wood boards and outdoor lath. Another common choice is manufactured lattice panels of either wood or vinyl. Several other more unusual materials may be available from your garden supply center, including rustic stakes and poles, peeler cores, and woven woods such as reed or bamboo. The amount of shade provided by an overhead is affected by the size of the materials used as a cover, as well as their spacing.

If you want your overhead to shed rain and snow, you'll need to install solid roofing materials such as asphalt roll roofing, or shingles. Because of the weight of these materials and the snow they will collect, a solid roof for an overhead should be designed by a professional.

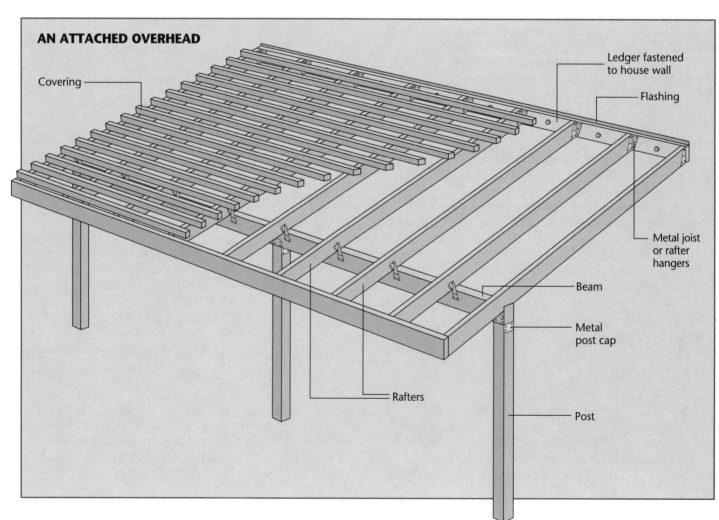

AN ATTACHED OVERHEAD

Covering

Ledger fastened to house wall

Flashing

Metal joist or rafter hangers

Beam

Metal post cap

Rafters

Post

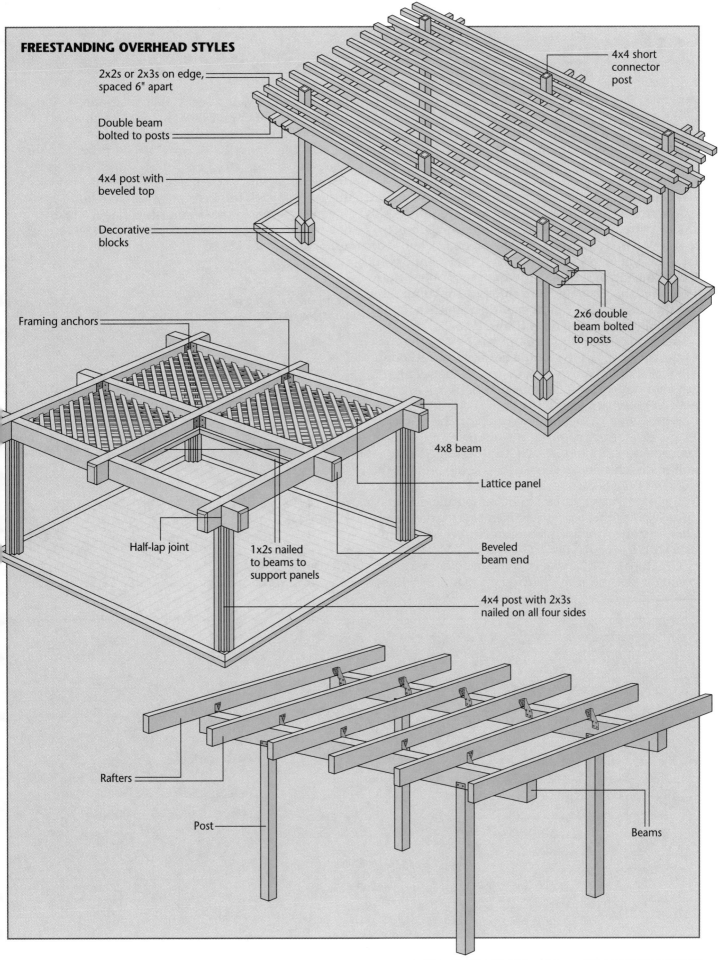

FREESTANDING OVERHEAD STYLES

2x2s or 2x3s on edge, spaced 6" apart

Double beam bolted to posts

4x4 post with beveled top

Decorative blocks

4x4 short connector post

2x6 double beam bolted to posts

Framing anchors

4x8 beam

Lattice panel

Half-lap joint

1x2s nailed to beams to support panels

Beveled beam end

4x4 post with 2x3s nailed on all four sides

Rafters

Post

Beams

BENCHES

Benches are very common multipurpose deck furniture. Not only a surface for sitting or lounging, they can also divide a deck into different activity areas, and guide foot traffic. Furthermore, they can become railings—but on a high-level deck make sure you use benches with backs.

When planning a bench, consider repeating design features from the railings, screens, and even the deck's surface pattern; this lends an orderly overall look to your deck. Alternatively, you may prefer a bench that doesn't blend in, becoming instead a focal point of your deck. Consider the three different types of benches: those that are integrated into the deck structure; those constructed as separate units, and then attached to the deck; and the freestanding, movable type.

There are certain standard dimensions for the conventional bench, which should be taken into account: The seat should be between 15 and 18 inches high, although sunbathing platforms may be as low as 6 to 8 inches. On a chair-height bench, the back should offer support at least 12 inches above the seat; the seat itself should be at least 15 inches deep. Angle an inclined back between 20° and 30°. Like railings, the backs of built-in deck benches can be capped; a cap protects the post ends from decay and, if it's set level rather than on an angle, provides a surface to hold food and drinks.

The legs or other supporting members for the bench must be sturdy, for adequate support, yet remain in scale with the bench design. If you're using 4x4s for legs, each pair can be spaced 3 to 5 feet; decrease this spacing if 2x4s or other lightweight materials will be used, or if the seat top needs additional support. Surfaced lumber should always be used for the seat boards.

If you want built-in benches, plan them at the same time as the actual deck. You'll need uprights to form pedestal supports for bench seats, or to serve as the frame for a bench's back; you can extend the deck's support posts up through the decking, or bolt vertical members to the joists. On the other hand, a freestanding bench can be attached to the deck at any time, using brackets or cleats.

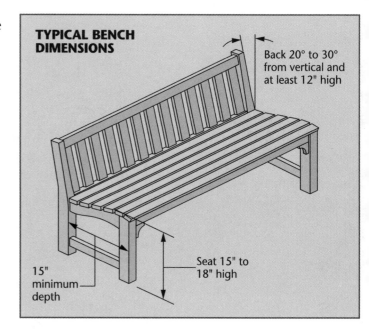

TYPICAL BENCH DIMENSIONS

Back 20° to 30° from vertical and at least 12" high

Seat 15" to 18" high

15" minimum depth

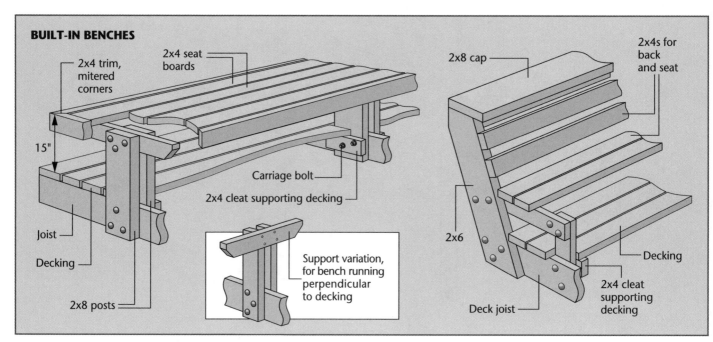

BUILT-IN BENCHES

2x4 trim, mitered corners

2x4 seat boards

15"

Carriage bolt

2x4 cleat supporting decking

Joist

Decking

2x8 posts

Support variation, for bench running perpendicular to decking

2x8 cap

2x4s for back and seat

2x6

Decking

Deck joist

2x4 cleat supporting decking

STORAGE

If you're looking for outdoor storage space, take advantage of the possibilities within your deck. If you have an enclosed bench, an easy way to create a storage compartment is to hinge a bench seat; you can use the interior of the bench for storage. Or, you can hinge a section of the decking, and suspend a plywood box from the joists underneath.

To turn a bench into a storage compartment, the entire seat can be hinged, or just part of the seat. For the latter, hold the hinged section together by fastening perpendicular braces to the bottom of the boards (use 1x3s, 2x2s, or 2x4s), as shown below. You'll also need to add 2x4 supports under the cut ends of the seat boards. Use corrosion-resistant hardware, and be sure to use sturdy hinges.

Building a storage compartment below your deck is also relatively easy. You can cut the decking for the lid so each end rests on the center of a joist or beam, or install 2x4 supports for the lid to rest on. The lid should be held together with braces attached to its underside. Use lengths of 2x2, 1x3, or 2x4, and fasten them to the underside of the deck boards with corrosion-resistant nails or screws long enough to penetrate about two-thirds of the way into the decking. You may want to add a diagonal brace: Use either a length of wood or a metal strap.

While a hinged lid is convenient, it's tricky to set the hinges so they're below the level of the decking, and the lid can be quite heavy. With a lid that sits in place and is lifted out for access, there are no hinges to set, and there's less danger of it falling on someone. Drill a hole for a finger pull, or add a handle—choose a type that you can recess into the decking.

The storage box below the deck should be made of exterior-rated pressure-treated plywood. Drill holes in the bottom for drainage. Fasten the box in place with galvanized wood screws; for extra strength, use carriage bolts or lag screws.

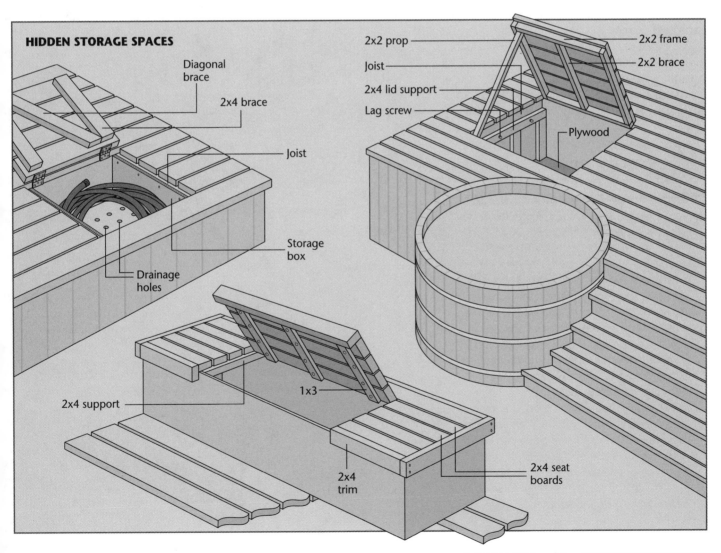

HIDDEN STORAGE SPACES

Diagonal brace
2x4 brace
Joist
Storage box
Drainage holes
2x4 support
1x3
2x4 trim
2x4 seat boards

2x2 prop
Joist
2x4 lid support
Lag screw
2x2 frame
2x2 brace
Plywood

PLANTERS

Aside from dressing up your deck, planters help connect the structure to the surrounding garden. And if you don't have much space in your backyard, planters allow you to enjoy a small-scale garden on your deck.

The starting point for most custom-built planters is the basic box; the designer's personal style is reflected in the surface decoration. However, regardless of your design, there are certain rules of thumb that you should follow in building a planter: Decay-resistant lumber, such as cedar or redwood heartwood, is best. Pressure-treated wood can be used instead, but avoid any treated with creosote, which is toxic to plants. For any plywood in the planter, use the exterior-rated pressure-treated type. If the planter will be made entirely of dimension lumber, use boards that are nominally 2 inches thick —actually $1\frac{1}{2}$ inches thick—for all but the smallest planters.

You can build a box quickly and easily by screwing the corners together; the joints can later be hidden under trim. Always use corrosion-resistant fasteners; for additional strength, you can apply waterproof glue.

ASK A PRO

SHOULD I WATERPROOF A PLANTER?

To give your custom-crafted planter the longest possible life, line its interior with a waterproof barrier to separate the soil from the wood. Two easy-to-use materials are heavy-duty plastic sheeting and roofing felt (tar paper). Completely cover the bottom and sides, staple the material in place around the top margin—the soil will hold the rest snug to the sides—then make slits over the planter's drainage holes. Or, you could paint the planter's interior with a waterproof, bituminous roof coating or roofing cement.

For longest-lasting protection, use a more solid liner fabricated to fit the planter's inside dimensions. You can make a fiberglass liner with materials from an auto-body or boat repair kit, or you can have a galvanized steel liner made at a sheet metal shop. Remember to include drainage holes.

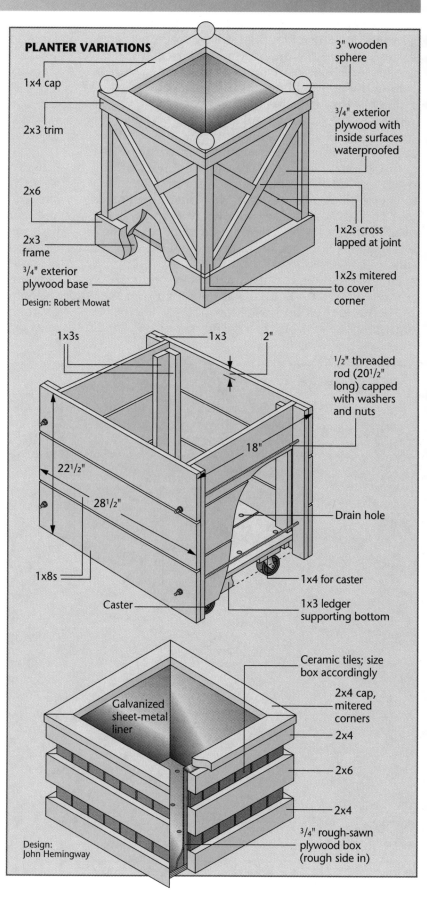

PLANTER VARIATIONS

1x4 cap
2x3 trim
2x6
2x3 frame
$\frac{3}{4}$" exterior plywood base
Design: Robert Mowat

3" wooden sphere
$\frac{3}{4}$" exterior plywood with inside surfaces waterproofed
1x2s cross lapped at joint
1x2s mitered to cover corner

1x3s
1x3
2"
$\frac{1}{2}$" threaded rod ($20\frac{1}{2}$" long) capped with washers and nuts
18"
$22\frac{1}{2}$"
$28\frac{1}{2}$"
1x8s
Caster
Drain hole
1x4 for caster
1x3 ledger supporting bottom

Ceramic tiles; size box accordingly
2x4 cap, mitered corners
2x4
2x6
2x4
Galvanized sheet-metal liner
$\frac{3}{4}$" rough-sawn plywood box (rough side in)
Design: John Hemingway

FINISHING

Exposed, unfinished wood can be damaged by the weather: It tends to warp, split, and crack from seasonal wet and dry periods; the sun's ultraviolet (UV) rays turn it gray; and water penetrates it, encouraging rot. Most experts recommend that decks be finished to help them withstand the weather, even decks built with pressure-treated lumber or with naturally decay-resistant lumber such as redwood or cedar heartwood. If your redwood or cedar decking contains any sapwood, apply a finish containing a preservative, since the sapwood of redwood and cedar is no more decay-resistant than any other species of wood. If you prefer the gray color of untreated weathered wood, choose a clear water repellent without UV protection.

If the substructure is pressure treated, a finish is not essential; the wood won't rot, and as long as the effects of weathering—warping, splitting, and cracking—aren't visible, they won't detract from the beauty of your deck. However, the substructure will withstand the effects of weather better if you apply a finish; this job is easiest to do before you install the decking.

Regardless of the kind of wood you're using, or the finish treatment you choose, it's best to apply the finish as soon as possible, to reduce the effects of exposure to weather. Leaving untreated lumber exposed for more than four weeks is not recommended. For best results, you can treat the decking before you install it; coating the ends of the boards is especially important because they absorb water many times more quickly than the surface. One way to be sure the ends of the boards absorb as much finish as possible is to coat them first, apply the finish to the rest of the board, and then coat the ends again.

Before you apply a finish, the boards must be free of mill glaze and sufficiently dry. Mill glaze is an impervious layer on the wood's surface created by the polishing effect of power tool blades when the wood is cut or planed. To remove it, sand the surface (try using a drywall pole), or use a mill-glaze removal product. Once this is done, apply the finish in a hidden area or to a scrap board (also treated for mill glaze). If it doesn't penetrate, allow the wood more time to dry (usually not more than one month) and test again. Or, choose a finish that can be applied directly to damp lumber. Always sweep or dust any debris off the surfaces before finishing them.

A variety of different finishes are available for decks, including water repellents, stains, and paints. Make sure the product you choose is suitable for decks, for the lumber you've chosen, and for the specific application. The horizontal surfaces of a deck (such as the decking) are subject to more wear than the vertical surfaces, and may require a different finishing product; check the product label. If you're using a brush to apply the finish, choose the bristle type appropriate to the finish: Use synthetic bristles for water-base finishes and natural bristles for oil-base ones. If the deck is raised, use drop cloths to protect the surrounding area from drips and overspray.

Water repellents: Clear water repellents, also known as water sealers, keep out water and help protect wood against warping, splitting, and cracking, but only those with UV protection prevent the natural graying of wood. Despite their name, clear water repellents will darken the wood slightly, especially with repeated applications over time. You can also buy water repellents with some pigment added, usually intended to enhance the natural tone of redwood or cedar decking.

A water repellent with a mildewcide is recommended, and is especially important if the product is oil-base, to discourage the growth of surface mildew. Water repellents with a mildewcide or fungicide are often called water repellent preservatives.

Stains: Semitransparent stains contain enough pigment to tint the wood, but not enough to hide the natural grain. Solid-color stains (also called heavy-bodied stains) contain more pigment; many are almost as opaque as paint. Semitransparent stains can last up to nine years, but solid-color stains usually have to be reapplied at least every two or three years.

With stains, the final color is a combination of the color of the wood and the color of the stain. A darker-colored stain will help mask the green tinge of some types of pressure-treated lumber.

Paints: Deck paints can mask defects in lower grades of lumber. However, they're harder to apply and maintain than stains—you may have to repaint your deck nearly every year to keep it looking good. Not all outdoor paints are suitable for decks, so be sure to check the label. Paints are not recommended for naturally decay-resistant wood, since they tend to trap water inside the wood.

NOTE: Both oil- and water-base finishes contain volatile organic compounds (VOCs), which are harmful to people and the environment. However, water-base products have much lower levels of VOCs, and are considered safer. Not all areas have regulations concerning VOCs, so read labels carefully.

PLAY IT SAFE

APPLYING A FINISH
Even when used outside, finishing products can be dangerous to your health. To protect your eyes and lungs, wear goggles and a respirator when applying any finishing product to your deck.

MAINTENANCE AND REPAIR

If your deck is getting on in years, it may look a little the worse for wear—and no wonder. Decking is especially vulnerable to damage: Rain and sun beat down on it; dirt and debris get ground into it; the spaces between the deck boards may fill with debris, impeding proper drainage; shaded areas below planters and deck furniture create perfect environments for mildew growth. If this is the state of your deck, don't despair: Sometimes a good cleaning, followed up with some regular, simple maintenance, is all that's required to make an older deck serviceable for many more years. You'll find cleaning and maintenance tips on the opposite page.

If you're facing more serious problems, such as warped decking, rotted posts, or joists or beams that need replacing, you'll find the information in this chapter helpful. Turn to page 90 for information on how to repair the decking. For tips on strengthening weakened railings and stairs, see page 91. Repairs to the substructure (posts, beams, ledgers, and joists) begin on page 92.

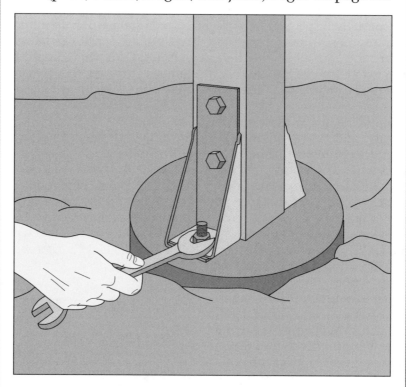

In this chapter, we'll guide you through some common deck repairs, from setting popped nails to replacing a post.

CLEANING AND MAINTENANCE

Regular cleaning is a key step in keeping your deck at its best; some other routine maintenance procedures are listed at right.

It's a good idea to get in the habit of sweeping the deck to remove leaves and other debris, and then spraying it with a garden hose to remove dirt. Use a hard spray of water to dislodge material that collects between butt joints in deck boards or between parallel boards, then scrape out whatever remains with a putty knife. Keep in mind that the stairs may need even more frequent cleaning, since they are probably the heaviest traffic area of the deck.

If you haven't cleaned your deck in a long time, it's probably not looking its best. Dirt tracked over and ground into it can eventually turn it dusty gray; in shady areas, mildew can build up and make the wood slippery when it's wet. But the hardest weathering comes from the sun's ultraviolet rays, which break down the wood tissue's lignin—a plasticlike polymer binding the cellulose fibers together. The result of degraded lignin is cellulose in minute strands, and these give boards a tired-looking gray surface. Stains may be caused by chemicals in the wood being drawn up to the surface through exposure to weather, or by iron from the use of ungalvanized nails or from contact with other metal.

If your deck is simply dirty, wash it with a sudsy solution of water and laundry detergent, scrub with a stiff fiber brush, and rinse with water from a garden hose. If you have a large deck, consider renting a power washer for the initial cleaning—it will help blast away dirt, and save you a lot of elbow grease. To deal with dirt, mildew, stains, and grayed cellulose all at once, choose a commercially available deck-cleaning product (sometimes also called a deck restorer) and follow the manufacturer's directions. Generally, you roll or spray the solution evenly onto the deck, wait a specified period of time (about 15 minutes), then scrub with a stiff fiber brush or broom, and rinse with a hose or power washer.

Many of these all-in-one products are much less hazardous—to both humans and the environment—than bleach or oxalic acid, which are the other products commonly used to clean decks. However, if you want to deal specifically with mildew or discoloration, you could use either chlorine bleach (for mildew) or oxalic acid (for stains).

To remove mildew, make a solution of 1 or 2 cups of household bleach per gallon of water, or buy a bleach-base deck-cleaning product. CAUTION: Never mix bleach with any product containing ammonia—a lethal substance will be created. Spray, roll, or mop the solution onto the deck, let it stand about 15 minutes, then spray it off with a garden hose or power washer. Don't scrub unless the product label recommends it; scrubbing can

☑ MAINTENANCE CHECKLIST

☑ **Move furnishings.** To give the deck a chance to dry thoroughly, periodically reposition any movable furniture, planters, or other accessories.

☑ **Inspect decking.** Clean any nail stains. Reset any popped nails, and replace badly splintered, split, or cupped boards (page 90). Check the spacing between boards; if any are spaced more tightly than $1/8$ to $1/16$ inch, slip an old handsaw into the cracks and work the blade up and down. Or, set the depth of cut on a circular saw to the boards' thickness, and run it between the boards.

☑ **Check railings or stairs.** Make sure railings and stairs are stable and in good shape; reinforce them if necessary (page 91).

☑ **Test for rot.** Insert an awl or the tip of a sharp knife into the wood; if it penetrates easily, or if the wood seems soft, and crumbles instead of splintering, it's probably rotten. Check for rot wherever two pieces of wood meet, on any surfaces where water may collect, and at ground level on wood in contact with the ground.

make the deck look worse. NOTE: Some experts recommend against using bleach on a deck because it has a tendency to break down the lignin that holds the wood fibers together. A deck cleaned with bleach will have a surface layer of loose fibers, which may keep any finish you apply from adhering properly.

To remove discoloration caused by iron or chemicals in the wood, use oxalic acid. You can either buy oxalic acid crystals at a home center or hardware store (mix a solution of 4 ounces of the crystals to 1 quart water) or use a cleaning product with an oxalic acid base. Apply the solution with a pressure sprayer, mop, or roller. Wait about 15 minutes, and then scrub with a stiff fiber brush or broom. Finally, rinse the deck with a hose or power washer.

Whatever product you use, work safely. Wear gloves and goggles when applying the cleaning product—and a respirator if you're using a pressure sprayer—or when scrubbing. Bleach can discolor fabric, so wear old clothes. Never mix different commercial cleaners, or mix them with any household cleaner, unless the manufacturer's directions tell you to. Also follow the manufacturer's recommendations to protect greenery around the deck; even those products that are least harmful to the environment in their final form may still cause damage to plants when undiluted.

REPAIRING DECKING

Periodically, your decking will require some minor repairs. Wood tends to swell and contract over time, causing nails to work loose, or "pop," so that their heads project above the surface of the deck boards. Resetting popped nails is a necessary part of regular maintenance for most deck owners. To do this, use a hammer and nailset to punch the nailheads flush or slightly below the surface of the decking. If some nails pop frequently, you can save yourself some work by replacing them with galvanized deck screws.

You may find that some boards are not level with those next to them, and need to be raised; and some deck boards may be cupped, warped, or rotten. Raising a deck board and dealing with a cupped board are described below.

If a board is only slightly cupped, you may be able to salvage it, rather than replacing it. However, if cupping is severe, or if a board is warped or rotten, you'll have to replace it. To do this, you first have to take up the board; pull out the nails or remove the screws. Or, if

nails have been used and you have easy access to the underside of your deck, you can hit the board from underneath with a hand-drilling hammer. (But if you intend to reuse the old board, use a block of scrap wood to protect the bottom surface of the board from the blows.) Next, cut a replacement board to the appropriate length and, using a nail as a spacer *(page 69)*, fasten the board in place.

ASK A PRO

CAN I REUSE OLD BOARDS?
If the decking surface is too damaged to be repaired by cleaning, but the boards are still sound, you can turn them over and reuse them. Remove a few boards at a time, turn them over, and fasten them in place again. Nail through the existing nail holes.

Raising a deck board

TOOLKIT
• Paintbrush for applying preservative
• Claw hammer

Inserting shims
If the surface of a board is not level with those around it, raise it by inserting shims underneath. Use either precut shims or a cedar shingle broken off to approximately the same width as the deck board. If you're using precut shims, coat them with preservative.

Insert one shim from each side of the joist; tap both of them in between the joist and the bottom of the board, using a hammer, until the board is even with those next to it.

Board to be leveled

Shim

Joist

Salvaging a cupped board

TOOLKIT
• Claw hammer to remove nails
• Screwdriver, screw gun, or electric drill
• Circular saw

Fixing a slight cup
Remove the nails and refasten the board with galvanized deck screws, tightening the screws enough to flatten the board. If this doesn't work, remove the screws and the board. Set the depth of cut on a circular saw to about one-third the thickness of the board, and make several lengthwise cuts on the back of the board. Fasten the board in place with galvanized deck screws. If this doesn't solve the problem, you'll have to replace the board.

NOTE: If you're having trouble removing nails, try the method suggested opposite, or use a nail claw or nail puller.

REPAIRING RAILINGS AND STAIRS

Railings and stairs must be kept in good shape to function properly—and safely. Inspect them regularly and make any necessary repairs promptly.

Railings: To replace any part of a railing—rail, cap rail, baluster, or post—the procedure is the same: Remove any fasteners holding the piece, cut a replacement, using the old piece as a model, and fasten it in place. For railing posts separate from the deck's posts, fasten a new one in place with bolts, lag screws, or framing connectors. For railing posts that continue from the deck's posts, follow the directions for replacing a post *(page 94)*.

To fix a loose railing post, counterbore holes through the post and the structural member of the deck that it's fastened to, and install bolts or lag screws. If the post needs further support, reinforce it as shown below.

Stairs: Strengthen the staircase with bolts or framing connectors where the stringers meet the deck *(page 65)*. If the stringers have moved out of position at the base, pulling the stairs away from the deck at the top, insert shims (cedar shingles) under the bottom of the stringers.

To replace a tread, first remove the old one; it may be attached with wooden cleats or metal angles, or in notches in the stringers. Cut a replacement tread and install it using the original method of attachment. Reinforcing a damaged stringer is illustrated below; to replace a stringer, first remove treads and any other pieces in the way. Then remove the stringer, use it as a template to cut a new one, and attach it to the deck and concrete pad as shown on page 65.

ASK A PRO

IS THERE AN EASY WAY TO REMOVE NAILS?
Hammering on the back of the board (the side opposite the nail heads) will loosen the nails, making it easier to pull them. You may then need to tap on the front of the board to expose the heads.

Reinforcing a railing post

TOOLKIT
• Circular saw
• Claw hammer

Adding a brace
Install a brace made of 2-by lumber between the post and the next post along the railing. Position the lumber diagonally between the posts, with the top of the brace against the weak post and the bottom against the next post. Mark the brace for length, and indicate the required angle on each end, then cut it to fit using a circular saw.

Choose the appropriate framing connectors for your situation *(page 25)*. Position the brace and nail the connectors to both the brace and the posts.

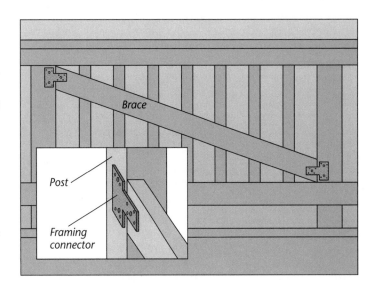

Reinforcing a stringer

TOOLKIT
• Circular saw
• Hand-drilling hammer
• Tape measure
• Combination square
• Screwdriver
• Electric drill

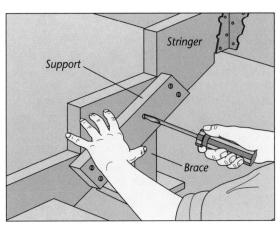

Installing a support
Remove treads or railing parts in the way, then cut a 2x4 at an angle to fit tightly under the damaged area as a brace. Position the brace on a board under the stringer and tap it into place with a hand-drilling hammer. Using lumber of the same thickness as the stringer, cut a support to extend about 6" past each side of the damaged section; shape it to match the stringer if necessary to cover the damage. Fasten screws in pairs along the length of the support, starting with two at each end; drill pilot holes first. Space the screws 10" to 12" apart (closer for shorter supports).

The substructure of your deck—joists, beams, posts, and ledger (if there is one)—should be inspected regularly to determine whether any repairs are required. Check that the substructure is stable and reinforce it where necessary, and look for warped, cracked, or rotted members that may need to be reinforced or replaced.

You can strengthen the structure of your deck by installing framing connectors at joints. Joints you'll want to check are between the joists and the beams, between the joists and the ledger, and between the joists and the rim joist. A wide variety of framing connectors are available, some specially designed for a particular situation; turn to page 25 for more information. Another way to reinforce the entire structure of your deck is to add bracing between the posts. Some varieties of bracing are shown on page 54; for instructions on attaching X-bracing, turn to page 57.

To reinforce a joist, solid blocking can be added between the joist and those on each side of it: Cut lumber for blocking to fit between two joists. (Use the same dimension wood as the joists.) Install the blocks in the middle of the span, offsetting them from one another and centering each block under a deck board. Face-nail through the joists into the blocks.

If a joist is rotten in a small area, supporting it just in that spot may be adequate. First, apply preservative to the rotten area. Then cut a 2x4 or 2x6 support long enough to extend about 6 inches past the damaged section on each end. Screw or nail the support to the side of the joist; stagger the fasteners every 10 to 12 inches.

If a greater portion of the joist is damaged, reinforce it with long supports; if it is beyond repair, install an entire new joist alongside the old one. Both of these procedures are described opposite.

If a beam is rotten or otherwise damaged, you'll need to reinforce it with supports (*opposite*) or to replace it (*page 94*).

To reinforce a weak post, you can bolt another post of the same dimensions to one side of it, or you can bolt a length of 2x4 to each side of it. For either of these procedures, drill holes through all the pieces to install the bolts. Instructions for replacing a rotted or otherwise damaged post are found on page 94.

To reinforce a ledger attached to the house, install additional fasteners. Drill pilot holes, spacing them about 16 inches apart and staggered. For a ledger fastened to wood framing, install lag screws; if the ledger is fastened to a brick or masonry wall, use expanding anchor bolts.

⏱ QUICK FIX

REMOVING ROTTEN JOIST ENDS

If the ends of cantilevered joists have rotted, you can cut them off. Carefully remove the rim joist, if there is one, and any deck boards in the way. Be sure to cut the joists far enough back to remove the rotten section of each one. Apply preservative to the cut ends, then install a new rim joist, if desired.

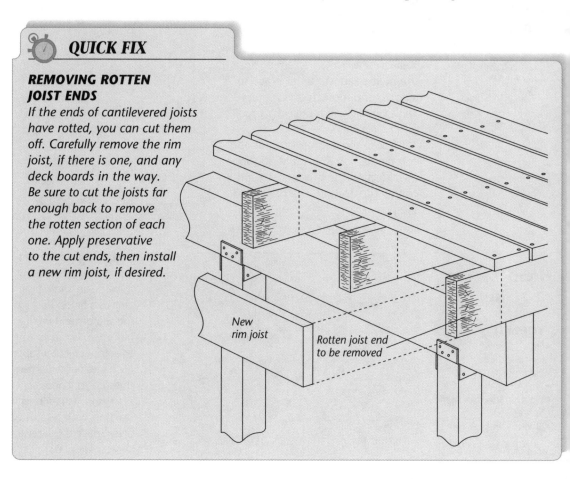

New rim joist

Rotten joist end to be removed

House jacks are either screw type or hydraulic. Whichever type you use, place a temporary support under the load as a precaution—this is especially necessary with a hydraulic jack, which may tend to slip.

Position the jack directly under the joist or beam. Place a 2x6 or 2x8 as a pad between the jack and the deck. Set the jack on a length of 2x10 or a concrete slab for a footing. Make sure the footing is roughly level before you install the jack—dig out the ground or, on a slope, add a concrete block underneath. Once the jack is set up, push it into plumb; check with a carpenter's level on two adjacent sides.

Extend the reach of a house jack *(near right)* with a length of 4x4; turn the screw adjuster for the final adjustments.

Raise the extension of an adjustable jack post *(far right)* to within a couple of inches of the surface being supported and slip the pin into the hole to lock it. Raise the jack the final few inches by turning the screw adjuster at the top.

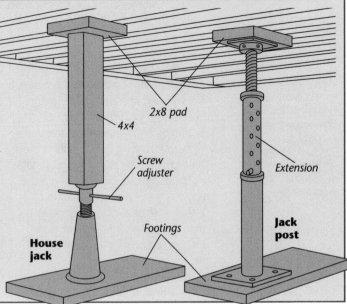

2x8 pad

4x4

Screw adjuster

Extension

Footings

House jack

Jack post

Reinforcing a joist or beam

TOOLKIT
- Claw hammer
- Jack
- Tape measure
- Circular saw
- Electric drill
- Wrench

Installing supports
Nail a short piece of 2x6 or 2x8 to the bottom edge of the damaged section of the joist or beam, to serve as a temporary pad for the jack to push against. Support the joist or beam with a jack positioned directly under the temporary pad.

For a joist, the supports should be cut from lumber of the same dimensions as the joist. For a beam, use lumber of the same width as the beam, but only half its thickness. Cut the supports about 4' to 6' longer than the damaged section of the joist or beam.

Position one support on each side of the joist or beam; drive in a few nails to hold them in place while you drill holes for carriage bolts through both the supports and the joist or beam. Stagger the holes about 12" apart along the length of the damaged section.

Tap the carriage bolts through the holes, install washers and nuts, and tighten.

Reinforcing an entire joist

TOOLKIT
- Tape measure
- Combination square
- Circular saw
- Claw hammer
- Hand-drilling hammer (optional)
- Jack (optional)

Installing a new joist
Rather than replacing a badly damaged or rotted joist, leave it there and install another one a few inches away from it. You'll fasten the new joist in place using the same method as for the other joists: They may be on top of, or butted against, two beams, or a beam and a ledger. Use the appropriate framing connector *(page 25)* to secure the joist.

Cut a new joist to fit next to the old one. Nail framing connectors to each end of the new joist, then position it about 3" to 4" away from the existing joist; the space will allow air to circulate and help keep rot from spreading to the new joist. With helpers, lift the joist into position. If the joist must sit on top of beams (or a beam and a ledger), pivot it to insert first one end, then the other, between the framing member and the decking. It may help to angle it slightly, then tilt it upright, tapping it into place with a hand-drilling hammer. This is a difficult task, so be patient. To raise the ends of a crowned joist, jack them up slowly until they're properly positioned.

Insert a 4x4 block between the new joist and the damaged one every 2'; face-nail through both joists into the blocks. It's best to leave out the blocks closest to the ends until you've attached the framing connectors, so you'll have room to swing your hammer. Nail the framing connectors in place, and remove the jacks.

TOOLKIT
- Tape measure
- Claw hammer
- Jacks
- Wrench (optional)
- Nail claw (optional)
- Hand-drilling hammer (optional)
- Crosscut saw or reciprocating saw (optional)
- Combination square
- Circular saw
- Carpenter's level

Installing the new beam

Support the joists with braces placed about 3' from the beam, on both sides. Nail two 2x10s together to make each brace and raise them on jacks, parallel to the beam, until they fit tightly against the joists. Position one jack every 6' to 8' and install additional safety supports.

Remove any pieces, such as stringers or railing posts, that are attached to the beam, and remove the fasteners or framing connectors holding the joists to the beam. Have a couple of helpers support the beam while you remove all the nails in the post cap. Tilt the post enough to slide the post cap out. Or, disconnect the bottom of the post as well, and reattach it after the beam is replaced. If the post is sunk into the concrete footing, cut it off and reinstall it as shown below.

Remove the beam, tapping it with a hand-drilling hammer, if necessary, to dislodge it. Or, saw it into smaller sections for easier removal. Cut a new beam from lumber of the same dimensions as the old one. Position the new beam between the posts and the joists; tap it into place with a hand-drilling hammer if necessary. Near each post, slide a post cap onto the beam. Tilt the post out of the way, then reposition it in the post cap. Plumb the post, then nail the post cap in place (below). NOTE: You can install T-straps at the joints between the beam and the posts instead.

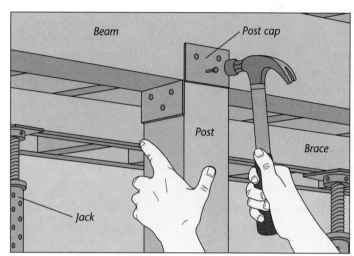

TOOLKIT
- Jack
- Prybar or nail claw
- Claw hammer
- Crosscut saw (optional)
- Hand-drilling hammer (optional)
- Tape measure
- Circular saw
- Carpenter's level
- Electric drill and masonry bit
- Wrench

1 Removing the post

Support the structure above the post with a jack, using an additional support for safety. Pull out any nails holding the post to the post anchor. To loosen the nails, pry the plate away from the post with a prybar, then hammer it back. If the post is set in concrete, saw it off flush with the top of the footing; if it's set on a nailing block, remove the nails holding the post to the block.

Remove the post; if necessary, tap it gently with a hand-drilling hammer to loosen it.

2 Installing a new post

The length of the new post will depend on how it's attached: If the old post was set in a post anchor, simply measure the post. Otherwise, measure the distance between the beam and the footing (or the nailing block on the footing) and subtract the height that the post anchor will hold the post above the footing or nailing block; cut the new post to this length. If you'll be using a side anchor as shown, the new post should span the distance between the footing and the beam.

The next step is to install the new post. If the old one was set in a post anchor, place the new one in the anchor, check it for plumb with a carpenter's level, and fasten it. If the old post was embedded directly in the concrete or set on a nailing block and the wood is in good shape, use the type of post anchor that can be attached to wood. If the old wood is not strong enough to accept a post anchor, use side anchors. Have a helper hold the post on top of the footing, and drill a hole in the footing to one side of the post, to fasten the side anchor to the footing. Insert an expanding anchor bolt in the hole, and fasten the side anchor in place. Plumb the post and fasten it to the side anchor with lag screws. Repeat to fasten another side anchor to the other side of the post (left).

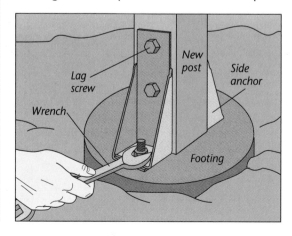

DECKS GLOSSARY

Actual size
The size of lumber after it has been surfaced, as opposed to nominal size.

Anchor bolt
Used to fasten wood to concrete; the bolt, usually J-shaped, is set into freshly cast concrete with the threaded end projecting above the surface.

Balusters
Thin, vertical members of a railing that divide up the space between posts.

Band joist
In a house, the framing member fastened across the ends of the floor joists.

Batterboard
A horizontal board held in the ground with a stake at each end; used to stretch string lines for laying out the deck foundation.

Blocking
Pieces of wood installed between joists to give rigidity to the structure.

Cantilever
To extend past the edge of the supporting member, such as a joist extending past the last beam.

Cap rail
Part of a railing; the horizontal member laid flat across the tops of the posts.

Cleat
A small piece of wood attached to one member in order to support the end of another. Cleats are often attached to stringers to support stair treads, or to posts to support decking.

Crown
The higher edge of a piece of lumber that is warped along its edge.

Dado
A channel with square sides and bottom cut across a piece of lumber.

Dead load
The weight of the deck materials themselves that the structure must be able to support.

Decay-resistant
Wood that is resistant to decay caused by fungi. Redwood and cedar heartwood are naturally decay resistant. Other woods can be pressure-treated against decay.

Dimension lumber
Lumber graded for strength and intended for structural framing. From 2" to 4" thick and at least 2" wide.

Elevation
A side view of a structure, showing vertical dimensions and relationships. An elevation section shows a vertical slice of the structure.

Expanding anchor bolt
A combined anchor and bolt used to fasten wood to masonry. The anchor bolt is tapped into a hole drilled in the masonry and a nut is tightened on the outside of the wood.

Face-nail
To drive a nail through one piece into another with the nail at right angles to the surface.

Fascia
Decorative trim installed around the edge of the deck to cover the rim joist, end joists, and ends of deck boards. Nonstructural.

Fasteners
Any kind of hardware used to fasten one item to another; typically, nails, screws, and bolts.

Flashing
Sheet metal used to protect a joint from water, such as between a ledger and the house. Can be bought already formed in a Z-shape.

Footing
The underground part of a concrete foundation. Distributes the weight of the deck.

Framing connectors
A wide variety of metal connectors used to join wood to wood, or wood to concrete. Form stronger joints than nailing.

Frost line
The maximum depth at which freezing can occur in a particular locale.

Galvanized
Fasteners that are covered with a hard coating of zinc that resists corrosion. Galvanized fasteners should be used for all outdoor applications. Hot-dipped galvanized are the best quality.

Grade
Ground level. Also, the slope of a lot, usually away from the house.

Ground fault circuit interrupter
A device that cuts a circuit in the event of a current leakage; required outdoors and in other damp areas. It is either built into the circuit or installed in an individual receptacle. Abbreviated GFCI.

Heartwood
The inactive wood nearest the center of the tree, as opposed to sapwood. Redwood and cedar heartwood is resistant to decay.

Kicker plate
A board laid flat on a concrete pad to support the bottom end of stair stringers. Attached to anchor bolts embedded in the pad.

Knee bracing
Short diagonal bracing fastened between a beam and the top of a post to add lateral stability.

Lag screw
A large screw with a square or hexagonal head that can be used instead of a bolt for heavy-duty fastening.

Lattice
A gridwork of wood strips; used for screens, skirts, and overheads. Can be constructed out of lath or bought preassembled.

Ledger
A structural member attached to a house or other structure; supports the ends of joists.

Live load
The load on the surface of a deck or overhead due to people, furniture, snow, etc.

Miter
A cut at any angle other than 90°. Also, to make such a cut.

Nominal size
The size of a piece of lumber when it is first cut from the log, before being surfaced. Lumber is sold by these sizes.

On center
A measurement of the spacing between a series of objects as measured from the center of one to the center of the next. Abbreviated "o.c." Spacings given in plans are generally measured on center.

Overhead
A structure such as a trellis built over the deck to give shade or privacy or to support climbing plants.

Pier
A block of concrete set on top of a footing to keep posts raised above grade. Can be cast in place or purchased precast.

Plan view
A view of a structure shown from above. A plan view of a deck shows the framing or the decking.

Plumb
Perfectly vertical. Also, to make vertical.

Pressure-treated
Lumber that has been commercially treated with chemicals to protect it from decay and termites. More effective than a brush-on treatment.

Radius-edge decking
Lumber specifically intended for decking. Milled with slightly rounded edges. Available in thicknesses of 1" or 1⁵/₃₂".

Rim joist
A type of joist fastened across the ends of the other joists, and intended to keep the structure rigid.

Rip
To cut a board parallel to the wood grain.

Rise
The vertical distance covered by a stairway.

Riser
The vertical part of a step.

Run
The horizontal distance covered by a stairway.

Site plan
Map of a lot showing the house, landscaping, and microclimatic features.

Skirt
A screen installed below the deck to hide the deck substructure or to protect items stored underneath the deck.

Sleeper
A length of pressure-treated lumber laid down and fastened to a concrete or brick patio to provide a nailing surface for decking.

Span
The distance a member covers from the center of one supporting member to the center of the next.

Stringer
The diagonal part of a stairway supporting the risers and treads. Can be notched or cleated.

Substructure
The framework of posts, beams, and joists supporting the decking.

Toenail
To drive a nail at an angle through one piece and into another.

Tread
The part of a step that is horizontal.

INDEX